Hints of Heaven

George William Rutler

Hints of Heaven

⁖

The Parables of Christ and
What They Mean for You

SOPHIA INSTITUTE PRESS
Manchester, New Hampshire

Sophia Institute Press
Box 5284, Manchester, NH 03108
1-800-888-9344

www.SophiaInstitute.com

Sophia Institute Press® is a registered trademark of Sophia Institute.

Library of Congress Cataloging-in-Publication Data

Rutler, George W. (George William)
    Hints of heaven : the parables of Christ and what they mean for you / George
William Rutler.
        pages cm
    Includes bibliographical references.
    ISBN 978-1-62282-232-4 (pbk. : alk. paper) 1. Jesus Christ—Parables. I. Title.
    BT375.3.R88 2015
    226.8'06—dc23

                                                                2014039785

First printing

To the memory of John Macquarrie,
Lady Margaret Professor of Divinity
in the University of Oxford

ᴥ

Contents

Hints of Heaven

Introduction

༄

Seeing, but Not Seeing

The kingdom of heaven is like treasure hidden in a field.... There was a householder who planted a vineyard.... The land of a rich man brought forth plentifully.... There was a rich man who had a steward, and charges were brought to him that this man was wasting his goods.... A man was going down from Jerusalem to Jericho....

These familiar lines open the most exquisitely austere and natural of all stories, the parables told by the Word who uttered the world into existence. The only proof I have of their literary superiority is that no one has ever been able to match them. Those who try are like a man standing before a masterpiece of painting who says, "I can do that," takes up a palette, and produces a greeting card.

A parable, to be pedantic, is a similitude employing a brief narrative in order to teach a spiritual lesson. In the case of Jesus, however, this definition is as unhelpful as it is accurate. John's Gospel has no parables, although it abounds in metaphors, but the three Synoptic writers, Matthew, Mark, and Luke, weave them in and out of the historical record, sometimes duplicating and even triplicating them. Depending on how one identifies a distinct parable, the number varies, but traditional listings name twenty-four in the Gospels.

I am aware that no man can match the Man who spoke the parables, and so to reflect on them requires a more profound consideration and a deeper decibel than commentary on ordinary literature. There are, however, two very serious, if not original, points to remember before embarking on even the briefest glimpses of these texts:

First, the parables of Christ are unlike other Eastern parables and the lesser stuff to be found in current "spiritual best sellers" in that they are not exotic. They do not distort or exaggerate nature in the way fables do. Kings are kings but not wizards, and rich men are rich but not omnipotent. The Good Samaritan carries the poor man to an inn; he does not fly him there on a carpet. The pearl of great price is valuable, but it is nothing more than a pearl. Jewish realism permits no such exoticism in the Old Testament, which contains five parables at most, depending on how one applies *mishna,* the Hebrew word for story telling.

Second, the parables really are what Jesus said they are: hints of heaven. Because the glory of heaven is too great for us to bear just now, Christ uses parables as delicate and veiled indications of our true homeland. Every culture has to some extent sensed that the glory of heaven is too bright for our eyes. The ancient Egyptians kept a veiled image of Ma'at, the goddess of Truth, in their temple at Saïs, believing that the actual sight of it would blind or even kill the viewer. The entire audience on the mount would have fled if Christ had plainly stated in His sermon that His kingdom was of another world. He saved that declaration for Pontius Pilate, who only shook his cynical head.

Seeing, but Not Seeing

Anything I say about the parables of Christ has this advantage over the perceptions of His original audience: the Resurrection is now a known reality, and the Temple veil has been torn open. And yet we are still unprepared for the weight of glory: "This is why I speak to them in parables, because seeing they do not see, and hearing they do not hear, nor do they understand."[1]

Understanding Christ's parables belongs to the childlike. The humble of heart recognize the lessons of the parables as they play out in the course of history. They surface in both the mistakes and the courage of the Crusaders, in both the glorious architecture and the inhuman tortures of the High Middle Ages, in the zealous missionaries and the haughty degenerates of the Counter-Reformation, and in the witness of the martyrs at the hands of the maniacs of the twentieth century.

The parabolic treasure is hidden in the concrete of Wall Street as truly as in a Galilean pasture. Every culture, advanced or backward, can understand a parable, because it offers a universally sought pearl. Mr. Caveman would have nodded some form of assent, as would the French heirs to Louis IX and Louis Pasteur and the English scions of St. Thomas More and Samuel Johnson.

Parables are often dismissed as too simple: Because a child can understand them, adults must yawn through them. And yet Christ spoke in parables. That fact is infinitely interesting and eternally salvific. In the face of worldly-wise criticism, one recalls the story of the tourist in Florence who sniffed that he was not all that impressed with the Uffizi's collection. A guard, heir to an ancient mandate to care for these treasures, replied in halting but intelligible English, "Here we do not judge the pictures; the pictures judge us."

[1] Matt. 13:13.

This point was lost on many of those who first heard Christ's parables, and Divine Providence permits us to view their example as a cautionary icon of confused pride: "When the chief priests and the Pharisees heard his parables, they perceived that he was speaking about them. But when they tried to arrest him, they feared the multitudes, because they held him to be a prophet."[2]

In their perverse pride, they would arrest a man for being arresting and would crucify Him for being a king. But in another world that is not so, and of this world the parables speak.

—GWR

---

[2] Matt. 25:45–46.

One

꙳

The Sower and the Seed

"A sower went out to sow his seed; and as he sowed, some
fell along the path, and was trodden under foot, and the
birds of the air devoured it. And some fell on the rock; and
as it grew up, it withered away, because it had no moisture.
And some fell among thorns; and the thorns grew with it
and choked it. And some fell into good soil and grew, and
yielded a hundredfold." As he said this, he called out, "He
who has ears to hear, let him hear."

And when his disciples asked him what this parable
meant, he said, "To you it has been given to know the
secrets of the kingdom of God; but for others they are in
parables, so that seeing they may not see, and hearing they
may not understand. Now the parable is this: The seed is
the word of God. The ones along the path are those who
have heard; then the devil comes and takes away the word
from their hearts, that they may not believe and be saved.
And the ones on the rock are those who, when they hear
the word, receive it with joy; but these have no root, they
believe for a while and in time of temptation fall away. And

as for what fell among the thorns, they are those who hear, but as they go on their way they are choked by the cares and riches and pleasures of life, and their fruit does not mature. And as for that in the good soil, they are those who, hearing the word, hold it fast in an honest and good heart, and bring forth fruit with patience.[3]

---

[3] Luke 8:5–15.

＊

The voice of Christ narrating the parable of the sower re-
sounds in Matthew 13, Mark 4, and Luke 8. Mark and Luke
depict Him escaping the crush of the crowd. Given my estima-
tion of the mass media, I relish the King James Bible's word for
that throng of people: our Lord avoids "the press."

Matthew joins Mark in painting a vivid picture — more typical of Luke's chromatic eye — of Christ using a boat as His pulpit
in order to be better seen and heard. Christ could whisper galax-
ies into being, but when He became flesh in time and space, He
had to shout to be understood. St. Matthew does not begin to
record the parables until his thirteenth chapter — as though the
Master had lately shifted into that mode of discourse as a form
of coded speech when his opposition was moving in to entrap
Him in His words.

His voice speaks now on the printed pages of the Bible, and
the letters pulsate; the words have preserved His message for
the edification of mankind. We examine them with the same
delight that prompted a precocious eleven-year-old Princess
Elizabeth in 1545 to write to her stepmother, Katherine Parr,
of the "most clever, excellent, and ingenious" invention of letters, for by them, "the mind, wiles, and understanding, together
with the speech and intention of the man, can be perfectly

known," and the original words "still have the same vigor they had before."

Elizabeth spoke of mankind in general, but the parables of Christ are the voice of the Man, the second Adam, speaking in decibels we can never fully comprehend outside of the revelation vouchsafed to the Church.

One way the Church interprets the parable of the sower is as a reference to her own mission: to prefigure on earth the golden ways of heaven. More practically, the parable addresses problems that have faced Christ's listeners through the ages. It is a concise synopsis of pastoral theology, in that Christ describes four types of listeners as four types of soil on which falls the seed of His words (although in the instance of one type, the "stony ground," they are not listeners but merely hearers).

The parable is about receptivity to His grace, more about the soils than about the Sower. The metaphor of the soils is a scriptural affirmation of our Catholic confidence in the existence of degrees of beatitude: there are different degrees of the earth's fertility, just as there is progression toward eternal bliss for souls in purgatory, and there are ranks of heavenly glory.

Christianity is not a limited corporation: its word is spread broadly. The Sower flings His grain widely, inevitably dropping seeds along the wayside, for He is willing to risk some to gain much. It is the principle of fertilization: the conception of a child is the articulation of the magnificent generosity inherent in marital love.

The "way side" onto which some seeds fall in the parable is the path of the proud, who consider the seed, the word of God, out of place or irrelevant. The sun will wither them up. The secular movements, philosophies, and fashions that have come and gone over the ages have failed to heed this curt warning of Christ's.

The Sower and the Seed

The stony ground in the parable is a thin layer of soil that masks rocks below. This soil is superficiality, the seductive cosmetic of obtuseness. Rocky soil is the senselessness of those who channel-surf through life, addicted to shallow entertainment and insubstantial celebrities who, as songwriter Noel Coward wrote in one of his lyrics, have a "talent to amuse" but not to save.

The stony ground is the tourist in Rome whom Louis Bouyer once observed to be more inspired by a Swiss Guard's plume than by the Blessed Sacrament. The birds get the seed that falls here. To identify those birds, I would suggest you simply read the front page of the daily newspaper. We laud those superficial personalities, and we choose them to lead a culture that is less their doing than ours.

The thorny ground in the parable offers no visible danger to Christ's word, but it hides deadly barbs. The seed that grows up among thorns grows in an illusionist religiosity: the smiley-face lapel button, the wall-to-wall carpeted church, the fey liturgy, the worship of youth. "The cares of the world and the delight in riches,"[4] as Christ explains in Mark's version of the parable, are the thorny soil of the New Age Gnosticism that is as old as Eden on the day the serpent slithered in. The seed that falls here is choked by illusions.

Finally, the seed that falls into the "good soil" in the parable makes a hybrid of heaven and earth; it is the indescribable conversation between God and man, the piercing beauty of the silent canon of the liturgy of life, the Christian drama that climaxed when the Temple curtain tore open. The seed takes root in the earth and flourishes, growing upward toward paradise.

[4] Mark 4:19.

Hints of Heaven

The seed itself is simply the seed. It is the blast of objective grace, arriving *ex opere operato* onto the soil of human subjectivity. In our present theological crepuscule, the Sower does not desire that we deform the good soil of the Church and her sacraments, but rather that we reform our own hearts to better receive the seed of grace.

A curate presiding at a funeral might toss soil onto the coffin and say, "Dust to dust, ash to ash." This gesture is an amen to the parable of the Sower. Christ told the parable so that each of us might let Him make of our graves what He made of His own borrowed tomb: a gateway to heaven.

Two

⁂

Tares in the Field of the Lord

"The kingdom of heaven may be compared to a man who sowed good seed in his field; but while men were sleeping, his enemy came and sowed weeds among the wheat, and went away. So when the plants came up and bore grain, then the weeds appeared also. And the servants of the householder came and said to him, 'Sir, did you not sow good seed in your field? How then has it weeds?' He said to them, 'An enemy has done this.' The servants said to him, 'Then do you want us to go and gather them?' But he said, 'No; lest in gathering the weeds you root up the wheat along with them. Let both grow together until the harvest; and at harvest time I will tell the reapers, Gather the weeds first and bind them in bundles to be burned, but gather the wheat into my barn.' " . . .

Then he left the crowds and went into the house. And his disciples came to him, saying, "Explain to us the parable of the weeds of the field." He answered, "He who sows the good seed is the Son of man; the field is the world, and the good seed means the sons of the kingdom; the weeds are the sons of the evil one, and the enemy who sowed them is the devil; the harvest is the close of the age, and the reapers are angels. Just as the weeds are gathered and burned with fire, so will it be at the close of the age. The Son of man will send his angels, and they will gather out of his kingdom all causes of sin and all evildoers, and throw them into the furnace of fire; there men will weep and gnash their teeth. Then the righteous will shine like the sun in the kingdom of their Father. He who has ears, let him hear."[5]

[5] Matt. 13:24–30, 36–43.

⁙

I remember with special affection a certain professor of mine who once said to a prolific rival: "I see you've written another book. What are you calling it this time?"

In the same way, commentators often lump Christ's parable of the tares in the field[6] (Matthew 13:24–30, 36–43) with His parable of the fishing net,[7] as though our Lord were repeating Himself or improvising on a theme. In the former parable, a man sows his field with good grain seed, but his enemy steals into the field at night and sows tares, a kind of weed, among that good seed. In the latter parable, a net thrown into the sea draws in both good fish and bad, like the good and bad seed.

While repetition is central to Hebrew poetry (the psalms echo verses by way of paraphrase, to intensify the feeling), no true disciple of Jesus can think that He simply runs out of imagination. The parable of the tares stands on its own, calling us to exercise patience with the human will as it exercises its God-given freedom.

Nothing is perfect in this vale of tears: all things are beautiful through the right lens, but God alone is perfect. Muslim weavers

---

[6] Matthew 13:24–30, 36–43.
[7] Matthew 13:47–50.

emphasize this point when they intentionally weave a discordant thread into every rug in order to avoid blasphemy. A prelate once grandly told those he was confirming: "All of us are sinners and have missed the mark, even I." The Church Militant here on earth basks in perfection from afar, while the Church Triumphant in heaven has already become perfect. Until the end of time, we are a mixed crop of saints and sinners.

Pope John Paul II said this in his public expressions of sorrow for the crimes of those who professed themselves to be Christians, as have the Polish bishops who publicly repudiated a massacre of Jews by townspeople during World War II.

Catholics in America might consider performing in the near future some public act of contrition for the recent plague of miscreant church renovators and the vulgarities visited on Catholic altars.

Sins are scandals, but sinners have always mixed with saints, and even the past sins of the saints should not surprise us. St. Augustine used the parable of the tares to confound the Donatists, ultrarigorous Christians who demanded the excommunication of their more lax brethren who had denied their faith rather than suffer martyrdom. The parable applies to contemporary Catholics who want their history airbrushed and who paint their saints with perfect complexions and capped teeth.

Evil is a presence inevitable, although not unavoidable, in consequence of the fall of man: "It is necessary that scandals come," Christ said.[8] The secular observer can miss this, for his mind is busy abusing religion for being religious and simultaneously faulting religious people for not being religious enough. Secular editors note more often that Hitler was baptized than they note that St. Francis of Assisi was also baptized.

[8] Cf. Matt. 18:7.

The parable also shatters the Calvinist solution to the problem of evil—that human beings are born depraved—for the bad seed comes *after* the good seed in Christ's telling. In the beginning, the field was good, and the first seed was good. Nature is not originally evil, and so we can reject Calvinism and Manichaeism and Jansenism and every modern pessimistic obfuscation of the sacramental life that gives grace to sinners. When the Master planted the wheat, He set in motion every baptism, marriage, and ordination. The tares were sown only the next morning.

The enemy steals into the garden when "good men slumber" (during His agony in the garden, Jesus found Peter, James, and John sleeping). The enemy never sows tares by daylight (Jesus was captured in the night and denied by Peter in the night). The enemy obscures lucidity with euphemisms and cloaks with pride the consciences of bright minds. Lucifer's light-bearing name is ironic, for his is the art of turning the light inside out, of casting high noon into midnight.

The Church is not our invention, and it certainly is not our possession. Therefore, we may not force it to conform to our grand visions of perfection. It was wrong to burn heretics, for while error has no rights, the erroneous do. Savonarola told the bishop who pronounced eternal damnation on him that he might damn him on earth but that God has the final word. If the tares are plucked violently, the very plucking could destroy the wheat.

Tares there are, but a harvest awaits. And this can be a consolation. For the saints are the wheat and, in the imagery of St. Ignatius of Antioch, can look forward to being ground for fine bread. All in good time. God is God and the source of the holiness of His Church. Its infallible witness against lies and its supernatural power over evil may well seem exasperating when they take the form of patience with sinners. But taken for what they are, with a dose of happy humility, they become a hymn:

"I have power to lay down my life, and power to take it up again."[9]

---

[9] Cf. John 10:18.

Three

༄

The Mustard Seed

"The kingdom of heaven is like a grain of mustard seed which a man took and sowed in his field; it is the smallest of all seeds, but when it has grown it is the greatest of shrubs and becomes a tree, so that the birds of the air come and make nests in its branches."[10]

[10] Matt. 13:31–32.

By a delicate symmetry, the parable of the mustard seed takes up just two verses of the Scriptures. In the eighteenth century "the least of all seeds," as the King James Version puts it, was such a convenient metaphor for next-to-nothingness that land was sometimes rented for the symbolic fee of one peppercorn, its minuteness a sign of royal largesse.

The Lord of Creation knew, and knows, more about the intricacies of His creation than any modern microbiologist or geneticist. His earthly contemporaries would have been confounded by the system that encodes in the first inkling of a life all that the organism will become. In modern bioethics, it is easy to lapse into a primitivism by claiming that a thing becomes alive only when it looks alive, but that contradicts genetic fact. A stem cell has as much claim on reverence for its life as a pope or a president or a Nobel laureate. A seed is alive, even if it looks like little more than lint, and the first cell of human life is alive, even if a clinician chooses to call it a blastocyst. The mustard bush is implanted with its mustardness and bushness even when it is a negligible seed, prey to rapacious birds, as the first cells of human life are prey to genetic engineers.

The mustard seed is a parable of the Church, nascent and fragile, yet inscribed by the Divine Word with all the saints and sinners, confraternities and schisms, shrines and hovels, golden and dark ages that will be until the Lord comes again. Zechariah prophesied it—who "has despised the day of small things?"[11]—as did Daniel when he saw a stone becoming a vast mountain.[12] Every cathedral and miracle and converted nation was in the breath of Christ when He said to the woman of Samaria, "If you knew the gift of God and who it is who speaks to you ..."[13]

The genetics of the Church as the Body of Christ totally befuddled those who measured greatness by size, whether they were Romans boasting the length of the empire or Jews hymning the height of the Temple. The little seedling did not seem to have much promise, and it seemed certain to die when it sprouted into a cross.

There remains a temptation to judge the Church by her size. If this means the number of converted souls, that is faithful to the parable and was commissioned by Christ Himself as He ascended. If it means only having the biggest basilicas, then the whole point is missed. The calendar of saints should remind us of the unreliability of appearances. Theirs is a greatness grander than size, and a prominence more cogent than popularity. A glance at Plutarch's *Parallel Lives*, written when the Church was just emerging on the classical scene, will reveal few names still recognizable today among all those once-famous Greeks and Romans. It will be the same two thousand years from now, when someone uncovers calcified copies of *People* magazine. There was nary an echo of Jesus' name in Rome the day He died.

[11] Zech. 4:10.
[12] See Dan. 2:35.
[13] Cf. John 4:10.

The Mustard Seed

The parable of the mustard seed takes account of the apparent insignificance of the early Church and declares that same Church's vitality. As the seed grows into the greatest of all the bushes, so does the Church grow from her beginnings into her full glory. This makes sense only in the light of heaven, for the Church's glory will always be brightest as a celebration of littleness. It is glorious when a million people gather to hear the pope, but only because the pope himself knows that he would never be more like Christ than if the whole crowd were to walk away, leaving him alone.

As a seed is nourished by the soil, so the Church thrives in indigenous cultures, transfiguring what is worthy, shucking off what is not, giving new vitality to old customs. The Druid's fire becomes the Yule log, Saturnalia shines brighter as Christmas, and the classical diocese and presbyter, vestal and pontiff are grafted onto an imperium that will never end. Here is a consolation, too: in the mustard bush all manner of birds will gather. Canaries are there, but there will be crows cackling along with them; vultures may share a perch with doves; common sparrows may feel a little intimidated next to peacocks; and for every wise owl you may expect a few cuckoos.

It is a little parable, this one about the mustard seed — deliberately so, I think. Its size teaches a sullen world a lesson in splendor. The Church learns as much from little verses as from long discourses; some of Christ's most pointed revelations are to be encountered in His asides. There is a lot of ecclesiology — not to mention botany and biology — to be garnered from the elliptical bits of God's Word that seem like breathing space between the grand panegyrics and pericopes. But the breath breathed is the breath that made the world.

Four

৵

The Yeast

*"The kingdom of heaven is like yeast that a woman took
and mixed in with three measures of flour until all of it was
leavened." Jesus told the crowds all these things in parables;
without a parable he told them nothing. This was to fulfill
what had been spoken through the prophet:
"I will open my mouth to speak in parables;
I will proclaim what has been hidden from the
foundation of the world."*[14]

[14] Matt.13:33–35.

*

In the heart of noisy Manhattan, when silence falls outside the window, I suspect something has gone wrong. St. Gregory the Great extended this feeling of alarm at silence to the moral order of the Church: "When one of his flock sins morally through his own fault, then he who is set above, because he kept silent, is responsible."

Healthy silence, however, should be the norm of the intestines and the soul. Parents, I believe, think their children are most attractive when they are quiet. Our culture of the chattering classes was the first to erase the traditional silent canon from the Eucharist. English poet Robert Bridges asked, "But who hath ever heard, who hath seen joy, or who shall ever find joy's language?"

I do not mean the pseudo-Buddhist Quietism of Molinos and Madame Guyon, who convinced many in the seventeenth century that spiritual heights are attained by total passivity. It was not a long stretch from that annihilation of the will to modern enthusiasms such as being "slain in the Spirit" and "holy laughter." These affronts to the economy of faith and reason simply betray an ignorance of the history of neurotic religiosity.

I do rejoice in that silence which is moved by perception of the holy. Fénelon's tinge of Quietism does not invalidate his words in the *Spiritual Letters*: "How can you expect God to speak in that gentle and inward voice which melts the soul, when you are making so much noise with your rapid reflections? Be silent and God will speak again."

The parable of the yeast, parallel to that of the mustard seed as an account of the way the Church will work, is about silence. Yeast has no decibels. A man quietly sows the mustard seed, and a woman quietly works the yeast into the dough. It is not that a woman cannot plant seed or that a man cannot work dough. (As a little boy, a French uncle of mine ran away from his birthplace in Versailles, hoping to become a pastry chef, the way American boys might want to run away to become cowboys or, in a reduced culture, basketball stars.) Our Lord uses these opposite little parables to join men and women in His great enterprise, and the King of heaven never condescends to the bourgeois mistake of thinking that maleness and femaleness are blithe biological accidents.

The yeast kneaded into the dough works so calmly that only a few shepherds in Bethlehem noticed the start of the process. This struck Phillips Brooks in 1868, when he had left Philadelphia for the Holy Land: "How silently, how silently, the wondrous gift is given!" The blaring shofar and brassy trumpet drowned out the voice of Jesus telling the parable in one verse: "The kingdom of heaven is like yeast ..." But saints caught the echo.

Christ says two things about His Church. First, the Church, like yeast in the dough, will change the character of the world, not its outward appearance. Bread is bread, leavened or not. The laws of nature will be unchanged, and men and women will look the same whether they spit at God or die for Him. But the worldliness of the world will never again be the same, nor will manliness and femininity be the same in mind and heart.

Grace, as St. Thomas Aquinas tells us, does not destroy nature but perfects it. There is an ocean between mystery and weirdness, between the holy and the exotic.

Then the parable tells how the Church, this kingdom, is to grow. The process is slow, but it is a procession with a purpose. Through the persuasive influence of personalities transformed by love, Christians will be the yeast that raises the culture through them: "It is no longer I who live, but Christ who lives in me."[15] And all this because of the Resurrection, for which yeast is an obvious metaphor, a metaphor the Western rite acknowledges by using unleavened bread for the Eucharist.

Without the yeast of grace, the human race is stale and dying. Christ wept for gorgeous Jerusalem falling flat on its golden ground. Human civilization has no intrinsic guarantees of progress. The prophet Daniel saw this in the idol whose head was made of gold, but whose body was made of brass and iron and whose feet were made of clay.[16] Christ alone can save culture. There will be dark ages and golden ages, but only Christ is the Light through them all. The primary voice for this in Christian life is the liturgy: It is a tradition, a continuity in outward forms, but electric with transforming power. Liturgy concocted by hobbyists, whatever romantic antiquarian claims they may make, lacks the leaven of Christ and falls flat. Josef Cardinal Ratzinger laments that "in place of the liturgy as the fruit of development came fabricated liturgy. We abandoned the organic, living process, with a fabrication, a banal, on-the-spot product."[17]

---

[15] Gal. 2:20.

[16] Dan. 2:31–33.

[17] Josef Ratzinger, preface to Monsignor Klaus Gamber, *Reform of the Roman Liturgy* (Fort Collins, Col.: Roman Catholic Books, 1993), back cover.

Hints of Heaven

The contemporary Church is suffering for her impatience with the way of yeast, which is impatience with Jesus Himself. He perdures, and His silent ways in a world of horns will rise up when every television network and newspaper and university and senate has drifted into the dust of ancient monuments and dead conceits: "The kingdom of heaven is like yeast ..."

Five

The Hidden Treasure

"The kingdom of heaven is like treasure hidden in a field, which a man found and covered up; then in his joy he goes and sells all that he has and buys that field."[18]

[18] Matt. 13:44.

⁂

Just as the parable of the mustard seed has its counterpart in the parable of the yeast, the parable of the hidden treasure is twinned with that of the pearl of great price. No twins are absolutely identical. Twinship can show up differences more vividly than an ordinary match of siblings.

The quest for the pearl is described as a hard and deliberate adventure, whereas the hidden treasure is stumbled upon by chance, and you get the impression that the man who found it was rather nonchalant. I do not say lazy, but he was casual, to say the least. If the man who roamed and worked to find the pearl was a man of sweat, this man was just lucky. He who found the pearl dug like a miner; the man who happened upon the hidden treasure could be the patron of those who win the lottery.

There is nothing inherently wrong with finding a treasure without working for it. Were it otherwise, no heir could be canonized, and many have been. I summon as a fresh and modern witness St. Katherine Drexel. Crudely put, the entire history of salvation is an account of how the bumbling and stumbling human race won the Great Lottery. Grace is gratuitous. As the Catholic knows, from the age of the apostle James to the moral tonic of Trent, faith without works is vain; but faith is faith, and as such, it is a gift. Should we make the mature examination of our souls in the second before the Particular Judgment, we may be astonished at how many times holy grace dropped into our laps without our recognizing it.

Salvation requires a response of the will, and in this parable, the response is deliberate recognition of the worth of grace. The man who chanced upon a hidden treasure acknowledged that it was a treasure. Not always does the believer appreciate the richness of the gospel. What is granted can easily be taken for granted, without the faintest amen. Otherwise our hymns in church would be louder, and the breast-beating at the *Agnus Dei* would bruise.

The pantheist should not gloss over this: The treasure was in one particular field—not in all of them. It was not the germ of every field that ever was. Nor was it somehow in the very nature—in the abstract "fieldness" of the field. The treasure, salvation—and there I have given the parable away—is a particular thing in a particular place.

The Church, before she is apostolic, is catholic; and before she is catholic, she is holy, and before all else, she is *one*. She is unique. This is easier to say today, now that the naive and injurious adolescence of ecumenism has matured. Now that religions speak to one another, we can say to others what was formerly speakable only among Catholics, and here it is: we affirm that the treasure of salvation is located (so to speak) in the Catholic Church. This is the case, not because of any inherent righteousness of Catholics, but because here is where God planted it. This Church is where Catholics—flawed human beings like their fellow men—can stumble upon salvation, and where anyone can do the same.

Knowing how upset sentimental people can become when thwarted, I had no qualms about allowing a parishioner to have her Highland terrier blessed in a non-Catholic church — in a ceremony that has virtually become a high feast in that denomination. But I still draw the line where blessing people is concerned. This is not because no other church's blessing could, under any circumstances, be of conceivable value, but because I know the Catholic blessing definitely gets it done.

Once this sacred deposit of faith is discovered by the gift of grace, the stumbler buys the field. Here is a moral challenge, for Jewish law required that anyone who discovered wealth inform its rightful owner: the "treasure trove" is the landowner's property. In His tumultuous ethic, Jesus condones the slyness of the lucky man, who is only a vagrant and not even a prospector, just as He positively commends the unjust steward and the unjust judge. The law is not condemned but fulfilled; in the casual words of a little parable, the raucous glory of heaven has slithered in through the cracks of time and space. The moral manners of heaven, whose homely tokens are a sense of humor and an appreciation of paradox, would seem to us far more perverse than this parable, and even horrible, without sanctifying grace or purgatorial refinement.

Heaven is not for the religious but for the heavenly, and heaven breaks through the bounds of earth when the clumsy soul chances upon the great treasure and takes it to himself with an exuberance that publishes the news in spite of all the proprieties of limited reason and habitual custom.

Six

⚜

The Net

"*Again, the kingdom of heaven is like a net which was thrown into the sea and gathered fish of every kind; when it was full, men drew it ashore and sat down and sorted the good into vessels but threw away the bad. So it will be at the close of the age. The angels will come out and separate the evil from the righteous, and throw them into the furnace of fire; there men will weep and gnash their teeth.*"[19]

[19] Matt. 13:47–50.

⁂

Without a sense of the Church, Jesus' parables can be reduced to exercises in moralism. Fundamentalist readers, or even those who would call themselves evangelicals, may miss the fundamentals of what Christ says about the Church. If your vision of Christianity is congenially de-historicized, the Church herself can seem peripheral.

In many of the parables, Jesus rivets the eye on the nature of the Church: what makes the Church work and how to discern her workings. In the parable of the net, His majestic countenance gazes upon the results. Visionaries may try to do that, but only the Divine Vision can see it for sure. This is why He walked with such a quick step and spoke with such vividness—dare one even say whimsy?—when He urged His disciples along the Galilean roads.

To those fishermen He described a shore with no sea, which is another way of describing a sea without a shore. I am not playing word games in saying this. The culmination of the Church will be a life with no ebb or flow, no waves, and no retreating of time with the tide.

The parable of the net disdains the romantic melancholy of Matthew Arnold in his poem "Dover Beach" (1867), which describes religious faith as withdrawing from the nineteenth-century world like a retreating wave. Arnold is morosely delectating on the fragility of confidence without the Church. The men of Arnold's time thought they had lost their faith because empires and combustion engines had distracted them. But they were simply paying the price for not having measured all things in the sacramental perspective of eternity.

When Christ told the parable of the tares, He was warning against haste in separating the evil from the good in the Church. This applies to all the contradictions of each churchly day: the ballet between the saint and the sinner, the screeching contest between Chartres and the modern suburban church that looks like a washing machine, the light of grace and the electric votive candle, a Bach cantata and the maudlin song "On Eagle's Wings."

The parable of the net is not less patient than that of the tares, as it might seem. They are simply two acts in the same drama. With the tares, we are told to put up with the present state, for things eventually will be sifted out. The net is the last act — the sifting out.

To use terms beloved of theologians with little apologetic skill, the net is teleological and eschatological. Whereas the parable of the tares is a discourse on patience for pastors, the parable of the net is the Pastor of pastors finally showing His hand. He pulls back the veil between time and timelessness.

And this is the meaning of the ineffable shore: in the Church, life is not concluded so much as it is consummated. The Church on earth is a prelude, a mystery as much as an institution, and indeed a mystery by the fact of being an institution. To sniff at the institutional Church is to forget that Christ did the instituting.

Gleams of the highest heaven are everywhere in parochial life, and that is why it is very shortsighted to use the term *parochial* as a slur. To walk from the baptismal font at the entrance of the church to the tabernacle in the sanctuary is to walk in quick step from Eden to the New Jerusalem. Much as one esteems and reveres academe, teaching in a university is tame compared with teaching in a parish. A professor is fishing in an aquarium, while a pastor is fishing in an ocean.

All kinds of fish are caught up in the net, but none is trapped in the end. All are dragged to shore—and not all are fit for the shore. This net is different from the linen sheet St. Peter saw lowered before him when he was told that all creatures on it were worthy to eat (see Acts 10:9–16). In the parable of the net, the universal call to holiness is distinct from universal salvation. Not all will be saved. Not because Christ does not will it.

The problem of the will is the problem of those who, by an act of the will, choose not to be with Christ. This refusal would seem breathtakingly impossible—except that we have seen the willfulness of the rogues of history. And each soul has known its own less worthy moments as it is pulled to shore beyond this world's horizon.

Seven

⚜

The Unmerciful Servant

"Therefore the kingdom of heaven may be compared to a
king who wished to settle accounts with his servants. When
he began the reckoning, one was brought to him who owed
him ten thousand talents; and as he could not pay, his lord
ordered him to be sold, with his wife and children and all
that he had, and payment to be made. So the servant fell on
his knees, imploring him, 'Lord, have patience with me, and
I will pay you everything.' And out of pity for him the lord
of that servant released him and forgave him the debt.

"But that same servant, as he went out, came upon one
of his fellow servants who owed him a hundred denarii;
and seizing him by the throat he said, 'Pay what you owe.'
So his fellow servant fell down and besought him, 'Have
patience with me, and I will pay you.' He refused and went
and put him in prison till he should pay the debt.

"When his fellow servants saw what had taken place,
they were greatly distressed, and they went and reported to
their lord all that had taken place. Then his lord summoned
him and said to him, 'You wicked servant! I forgave you

all that debt because you besought me; and should not you have had mercy on your fellow servant, as I had mercy on you?' And in anger his lord delivered him to the jailers, till he should pay all his debt. So also my heavenly Father will do to every one of you, if you do not forgive your brother from your heart."[20]

[20] Matt. 18:23–35.

＊

St. Peter was an impetuous man, unlike most of his successors. But the parable of the unmerciful servant came to be told through one of those rare instances in which he showed a curious reserve. Leading up to it, in Matthew 18:1–20, the disciples ask our Lord who among them will be greatest in heaven. The question may have been first suggested by Peter—or perhaps the others ask it ironically in oblique reference to him.

Our Lord famously replies by calling over a little child and telling the disciples that they will be great in the kingdom to come only insofar as they become as simple as little children—and deal patiently and mercifully with sinners.

Peter can no longer keep silent, and asks plaintively: How often do I have to forgive? *Usquequo Domine?* Seven times? (This is not the most promising start from the father of all the world's confessors.) Peter is no doubt hoping to appear magnanimous. But his bourgeois arithmetic provokes the Master's royal calculus: seventy times seven. That is—without limit.

Christ is a king and rules a heavenly city. Peter would suburbanize his Master. (I speak metaphorically here, having lived for forty years in Westchester County as happily as in Galilee.) Peter's kind of king would be more Dutch than Oriental, with Peter as the obliging prime minister. He wants a simple, numerical rule he can consult and enforce. But He whose kingdom is not of this world will have none of that; He wants not numbers, but hearts. His eternal wisdom not only requires forgiveness; it also demands that the forgiver try to convert the offender.

Forgiven a huge debt by his king, the servant in the parable refuses to forgive a small debt owed to him by another, lesser servant. He is merciless because he is unconverted himself. While translating ancient currencies is notoriously hard, in terms of modern, union-scale wages, the servant may have owed the king $4.5 billion. (I have the ambiguous conversion charts.) The sum does not seem exaggerated, given government waste in any period. To be in charge of such a budget, the servant must have been some sort of satrap, the equivalent of a highly placed civil servant in our federal Department of Education.

One could tame the parable by concluding that it simply means we must forgive others. That may be how it is preached from some pulpits—while the congregation tolerantly glances through the parish bulletin. A man fumed to me that his pastor ordered his parishioners to forgive Osama bin Laden. Is that the burden of the parable? Not quite. City people have to be tougher than suburbanites (the metaphor again), and Christ is King of the heavenly Jerusalem, so He is tougher than all of us. Jesus is streetwise, and His streets are paved with gold. Let's ask: Need we forgive the most despicable of people?

First, answer the question like a saint—for saints consider themselves the most despicable. (The fact that they are so wrong about themselves highlights that they are so right about everyone else.) Now answer the question like Christ, whose blood absolved us. I have no chart to convert His blood into modern dollars, but I do know it was poured out freely at great cost. It is ours for the asking, but *only at the price of everything that prevents our asking.* That was the dilemma of the two thieves crucified with Christ. Only one was generous enough to ask.

There is no reason to forgive anyone unless it is done with enough humility to inspire humility in the one who is forgiven. Forgiveness is not an easy platitude offered to the smug; nor is it an aggressive display of pacifism. Jejune philanthropy situates me in a moral suburb that is bucolic for a day and hell for eternity.

"Let the wicked forsake their way, and the unrighteous their thoughts; let them return to the LORD, that he may have mercy on them, and to our God, for he will abundantly pardon." So spoke Isaiah, as elsewhere, in consort with the psalmist and St. John.[21]

All of us are indebted to God; none of us has enough to pay the debt. God is willing to forgive the debt, but the condition of the absolution is that we grant it to those around us. The moral deficiency in the unmerciful servant is hinted at in the way he has to be "brought" before the king. A man so niggardly lacks the moral elegance to be anything more than a petit bourgeois outside the gates of Zion.

He who was forgiven much forgave little, for it is easier to leash sin than to unleash grace. Unctuous words of forgiveness will not populate heaven with luminous saints who once had been the most lurid sinners. Efficacious grace must be a chain reaction. God wills that all be saved, but pride holds us prisoner. "Forgive us our debts as we forgive our debtors."[22] The selfishness of those who damn themselves turns the Lord's Prayer into the Devil's Prayer.

---

[21] Isa. 55:7; cf. 1:18; Ps. 130:7–8; 1 John1:9.
[22] Cf. Matt. 6:12.

Eight

༈

Laborers in the Vineyard

"[T]he kingdom of heaven is like a householder who went out early in the morning to hire laborers for his vineyard. After agreeing with the laborers for a denarius a day, he sent them into his vineyard. And going out about the third hour he saw others standing idle in the market place; and to them he said, 'You go into the vineyard too, and whatever is right I will give you.' So they went. Going out again about the sixth hour and the ninth hour, he did the same. And about the eleventh hour he went out and found others standing; and he said to them, 'Why do you stand here idle all day?' They said to him, 'Because no one has hired us.' He said to them, 'You go into the vineyard too.'

"And when evening came, the owner of the vineyard said to his steward, 'Call the laborers and pay them their wages, beginning with the last, up to the first.' And when those hired about the eleventh hour came, each of them received a denarius. Now when the first came, they thought they would receive more; but each of them also received a denarius. And on receiving it they grumbled at the householder, saying, 'These last worked only one hour, and you have made them equal to us who have borne the burden of the day and the scorching heat.'

"But he replied to one of them, 'Friend, I am doing you no wrong; did you not agree with me for a denarius? Take what belongs to you, and go; I choose to give to this last as I give to you. Am I not allowed to do what I choose with what belongs to me? Or do you begrudge my generosity?'

"So the last will be first, and the first last."[23]

---

[23] Matt. 20:1–16.

᾿᾿

Lord Palmerston, or certainly some such confident Victorian, said: "If you do well here, you'll do well there." Many Christians may now approve that outline of salvation, although its lightweight account of grace and goodness is the seductive Pelagian heresy. The rich young man who had kept the commandments and asked our Lord to finish the picture had more than a tinge of it.[24] After he had walked away, our Lord uttered some strong words about the weight of wealth, leading Peter to ask: "Look, we have left everything and followed you. What then will we have?"[25] The parable of the laborers in the vineyard is our Lord's response.

The Master pays workers a fair wage agreed upon, but those who are hired at the end of the day get paid as much as those who toiled from the start. First Christ assures His followers that they will be compensated. Then He delicately rebukes Peter's bargaining spirit. The apostles had been Christ's first followers and were privileged because of it, but many latecomers would receive no less an abundance of glory. They had come out of trust and not calculation. So clericalism and meretricious religiosity come crashing down.

[24] See Matt. 19:16–22.
[25] Matt. 19:27.

Hints of Heaven

It has become something of a trend in pious corners for well-intentioned entrepreneurs to declare that they want to die poor so that they might become saints. Dying poor guarantees nothing except a modest funeral. Spoken carelessly, this avowal carries the subtle scent of the calculator; it is a little like the remark I once heard from a cleric who said he had become a priest to save his soul. No one becomes a saint by wanting to be one; it happens by loving God. No priest will save his own soul unless his first and selfless desire is to save other souls. Otherwise, the profession of faith becomes a demeaning little question whispered behind the gauzy curtain of unction: "What's in it for me?"

Self-love is proper, and so is the love of God for what He does for us. But both are counterfeit kinds of happiness until they result in the eternal happiness that is love of God, purely because He is God. St. Bernard said it more mellifluously in his Latin, but the point is this: if a man gives up all that he has in order to have a room with a view in the Everlasting Halls, he will not be very satisfied there for all eternity. Love has to be the calculus of a life lived forever with Him who is Love. Without it, we have bargained for nothing more than an Islamic or Mormon paradise, which after a human lifetime would begin to feel like hell.

All is fair in God's covenants, and He pays the early workers the full sum agreed upon. They are icons of free will, for the Master lets them call the shots. They rule the market, and He goes by the rule. But at the end of the day, the late arrivers are paid before the others because the rule states only that payment is to be made, not when it is to be paid. The laborers hired last are paid first because of the gratitude they show in their importunity. The Lord who loves a generous giver loves no less a generous receiver. Humans were made to give God delight, and nothing delights Him more than human delight in Him. Here is courage for the convert.

Christ hints at Peter's future dignity in Rome when He speaks this parable especially to him. It trained Peter for the primacy before it tutored us. No apostle can be what an apostle is meant to be if he begrudges anyone else an abundance of grace. Many popes have a high place in heaven—not because they were popes but because they did in the papacy what any anonymous saint did in any anonymous situation: they pleased God by loving others with a spark of the Love that brought them into being. That the first shall be last is our Lord's reminder that many popes and princes and billionaires, all candidates for glory, opted for its opposite.

Liberation theology, which not long ago bewitched comfortable university salons with its romantic misreading of justice, has quickly become a cultural vignette. It misinterpreted this parable, so that all who were first became last, and all who were last became first.

Actually, many who were first stay first, and many who were last stay last. The status is irrelevant. Motive is all. Christ next says bluntly, "Behold, we go up to Jerusalem."[26] That is where the vineyard is, and in the vineyard is the cross. Those who arrived at the end of the day missed the raw sun glistening on the Galilean lake and did not hear the leper cry with joy; nor did they glimpse Jesus transfigured on the Mount. For them at day's end, there is only the cross and the cross and the cross ... and then the Light.

---

[26] Matt. 20:18, Douay-Rheims Bible.

Nine

⚜

The Two Sons

"A man had two sons; and he went to the first and said,
'Son, go and work in the vineyard today.' And he answered,
'I will not'; but afterward he repented and went. And he
went to the second and said the same; and he answered, 'I
go, sir,' but did not go. Which of the two did the will of his
father?" They said, "The first." Jesus said to them, "Truly,
I say to you, the tax collectors and the harlots go into the
kingdom of God before you. For John came to you in the
way of righteousness, and you did not believe him, but the
tax collectors and the harlots believed him; and even when
you saw it, you did not afterward repent and believe him."[27]

[27] Matt. 21:28–32.

When the priestly caste and the constituted authorities challenge His claims, Christ throws off any mantle of harmless philanthropy in which the lukewarm souls would cloak Him. Here is no romantic Sage of Galilee (as David Flusser describes in his book of that name).

At the age of twelve, Jesus had called this Temple His Father's house. Now that intimation of divinity becomes more discomfiting to the Temple's clerical caretakers. The priests and the elders had made many promises to God; the Law was full of them, and it would break hearts to think that there would be no Messiah to make them all worthwhile. But John had preached the coming of the Messiah, and they had failed to believe him.

As the atmosphere grows tense in Jerusalem, the problematic Rabbi from Nazareth will not be intimidated by their disdain for Him. He attacks — with the parable of the two sons.

There were two sons who promised to help out in the vineyard. The scene is more intimate than the earlier parable of the laborers,[28] where the vineyard was grander and the owner richer. The moral focus here is narrowed to a delicate examination of conscience. One son tells his father flat out that he will not work

---

[28] Matt. 20:1–16.

for him. He is no hypocrite, but that alone will not get him a day on the Calendar of Saints. A man may follow his conscience all the way to heaven, but he may follow it all the way to hell, too. Publicans and harlots will go to heaven before the self-righteous hypocrites, but not because of publicanism and harlotry. They repented and believed. The son is saved because eventually he does go to work.

The second son makes florid promises and is a darling for it, but he does not mean what he says. Here is every dishonest politician on inauguration day, every spoiled youth making marriage vows with the ink still wet on a premarital agreement about dividing property. Here too is the sad fellow who became a priest to please his family or to hide some moral pathology. St. Ignatius knew his spiritual army needed men brave as their intentions and so in the *Spiritual Exercises* he wrote, "One must not swear, neither by Creator nor by creature, unless it be with truth, necessity, and reverence."

As sincerity is not salvific in itself, neither is the keeping of a promise. John the Baptist lost his head because Herod kept his promise. Herod's tragedy was the oppressive smallness of his moral universe. So too with the chief priests and the elders: within the Temple precincts, their own voices sounded to them like the echo of God.

Jesus broke the illusion and damned the acoustics: "The baptism of John: was it from heaven or from men?"[29] The question set a trap for them, and rather than stumble into it by inadvertent honesty, they affected agnosticism: "We cannot tell." In their case, this meant they *could* tell but would not, and the very utterance made each of them like the second son, who made a

---

[29] Cf. Matt. 21:25.

promise now but did as he pleased later. Father Vincent McNabb said that agnosticism solves no mysteries but only shelves them: "When agnosticism has done its withering work in the mind of man, the mysteries remain as before; all that has been added to them is a settled despair."

Perhaps the second son was not completely dishonest in making his promise. He may have thought the promise would be easy to keep. There was even a reverence about him lacking in his brother, for he called his father Sir, but his brother did not. He would have managed had the vineyard been a botanical garden with pleasant paths and subdued horticulturists nodding hello. That is the clericalist's fantasy of the Church. It must be kept up even if it means pretending there are no weeds. Bromidic pieties about hushing up scandals and being lenient toward the reprobates "for the good of the Church" are designed for the good of those who have made promises with a conscience too delicate for reality. St. Gregory the Great upbraided those of nervous faith by saying that the truth must not be suppressed for fear of scandal.

The chief priests and the elders wanted everyone to get along together, keeping their perks of office, of course. The Temple, whose smoke and sacrifices should have been as dreadfully wonderful as Jacob's dream, had instead become rather charming to them. That was their spiritual death. Christ broke that agnostic spell with His parable of the two sons. Promises are not enough, nor is an honest wallowing in disobedience. God in Christ will forgive any act for the asking, but there must be the act of asking, and the one asked must be Christ.

Christ's words to the chief priests and the scribes about His cousin John were preparation for what they would have to decide about Peter when he preached on Pentecost: "Repent, and be baptized every one of you in the name of Jesus Christ so that your sins may be forgiven; and you will receive the gift of the Holy Spirit."[30]

[30] Acts 2:38.

Ten

✳

The Wicked Husbandmen

"*Hear another parable. There was a householder who planted a vineyard, and set a hedge around it, and dug a wine press in it, and built a tower, and let it out to tenants, and went into another country. When the season of fruit drew near, he sent his servants to the tenants, to get his fruit; and the tenants took his servants and beat one, killed another, and stoned another. Again he sent other servants, more than the first; and they did the same to them. Afterward he sent his son to them, saying, 'They will respect my son.' But when the tenants saw the son, they said to themselves, 'This is the heir; come, let us kill him and have his inheritance.' And they took him and cast him out of the vineyard, and killed him. When therefore the owner of the vineyard comes, what will he do to those tenants?*" *They said to him,* "*He will put those wretches to a miserable death, and let out the vineyard to other tenants who will give him the fruits in their seasons.*"

Jesus said to them, "*Have you never read in the scriptures:*

'The very stone which the builders rejected
has become the head of the corner;
this was the Lord's doing,
and it is marvelous in our eyes'?

"Therefore I tell you, the kingdom of God will be taken
away from you and given to a nation producing the fruits of
it. And he who falls on this stone will be broken to pieces;
but when it falls on any one, it will crush him."

When the chief priests and the Pharisees heard his
parables, they perceived that he was speaking about them.[31]

[31] Matt. 21:33–45.

The Temple officials in Jerusalem could not have enjoyed the parable of the two sons, which they recognized was aimed at them. And now the common crowd relishes the discomfort of the sanctimonious, eager to see what will happen next. They do not jeer, for this is not a college debate, but you can see them grinning at the spectacle of those pompous men nervously fiddling with their long tassels—on which they know the Nazarene casts a cold eye.

These dignitaries have long enjoyed the acoustics of the Temple precincts. The marble corridors gave their voices a timbre that made them sound—to their own ears at least—like the oracles of God. They were men of the stained-glass voice before there was stained glass. And yet when Jesus flashes words of lightning, they are left all aquiver, like overweight and overage prizefighters sagging on the ropes. Worse, Jesus makes his verbal sparring look effortless.

He quietly says, "Hear another parable," and they grimace.

This time He speaks of a tidy vineyard, and they know what He means. They have been tending the House of Israel, and living very well by doing it poorly. It may have been said unfairly of the Quakers that they went to Pennsylvania to do good and also did well, but it was much the case with these priests and elders. As tenant farmers, stewards by divine decree since the first garden was planted east of Eden, they gradually assumed proprietary airs over their legacy. Through thick moral lenses, their opinion and God's truth were to them one and the same.

God's vineyard is salvation history, and they have commandeered it—passing off their obscurantism as His light. Hence the parable is of the *wicked* husbandmen—rather than stubborn or selfish or misguided. They had long rejected the sons of God,[32] and now they are rejecting the very Son of Man. Christ's awful wailing over Jerusalem, which kills the prophets,[33] writes this parable in tears. Christ is the cornerstone of the heavenly Jerusalem, and rejection of Him will bring its magnificently built earthly symbol crashing down on its wicked tenants—canceling all access to that City which was not made with hands.

God has bestowed unspeakably great privileges on His people, and that is truer of us than of any generation: "[M]any prophets and righteous people longed to see what you see, but did not see it, and to hear what you hear, but did not hear it."[34]

But notice how our culture rejects the palpable evidence of miracles. The existence of saints is surely more taxing to the cynical observer than any miracles they perform. Still, it is wonderful how the inquisitive media, even in news reports about a pope declaring a new saint, almost completely black out information about the miracles that paved the way for the saint's canonization. You would expect these to be mentioned in the secular press, if only out of morbid curiosity or increased sales—but they are not. Similarly, the lives of the saints, the

---

[32] 2 Chron. 36:15–16.
[33] Matt. 23:37.
[34] Matt. 13:17.

The Wicked Husbandmen

most vivid personalities in human history, are conspicuous by their absence from the university curriculum. Thomas More is the only saint mentioned in a sociology textbook used in a major New York university, and all the book says about him is that he was the "Father of Euthanasia." The authors apparently did not get More's joke: his *Utopia* describes an "ideal" society that practices euthanasia—but *utopia* is Greek for "nowhere," and the book is satire.

The parable of the wicked husbandmen does not let this kind of nonchalance in the face of grace get off lightly. However infrequently it may be declaimed from the pulpits of happy-clappy churches, this is what the parable tells us: the Lord shall be "revealed from heaven with his mighty angels in flaming fire, inflicting vengeance on those who do not know God and on those who do not obey the gospel of our Lord Jesus. These will suffer the punishment of eternal destruction, separated from the presence of the Lord and from the glory of his might."[35]

A self-help book for business leaders proposes Jesus as the greatest model for management techniques. Its shrewd insights about human relations and motivating people do not claim to be theological. But even as helpful advice, it attains the level of magnificent grotesquery:

> Jesus' plan for transition was the most successful in history.... His associates did not want to see him go, but they were forewarned. They performed beautifully after Jesus was taken from them, pushing the program forward to unimagined success. Jesus planned well for his succession. So should you. Your company and your associates deserve it.

[35] 2 Thess. 1:7–9.

The neatness of the metaphor notwithstanding, the parables are not lessons in social management. The calamity of wicked husbandry was its ignorance of divine succession. As a result, the tenants would kill the one Man who needs no successor, for He is the eternal Son of the everlasting Father, and He dwells in His followers by sanctifying grace.

Eleven

༈

The Marriage of the King's Son

When the chief priests and the Pharisees heard his parables,
they perceived that he was speaking about them. But when
they tried to arrest him, they feared the multitudes, because
they held him to be a prophet.

And again Jesus spoke to them in parables, saying, "The
kingdom of heaven may be compared to a king who gave a
marriage feast for his son, and sent his servants to call those
who were invited to the marriage feast; but they would not
come. Again he sent other servants, saying, 'Tell those who
are invited, Behold, I have made ready my dinner, my oxen
and my fat calves are killed, and everything is ready; come
to the marriage feast.' But they made light of it and went
off, one to his farm, another to his business, while the rest
seized his servants, treated them shamefully, and killed them.
The king was angry, and he sent his troops and destroyed
those murderers and burned their city. Then he said to his
servants, 'The wedding is ready, but those invited were not
worthy. Go therefore to the thoroughfares, and invite to the
marriage feast as many as you find.' And those servants

went out into the streets and gathered all whom they found, both bad and good; so the wedding hall was filled with guests.

"But when the king came in to look at the guests, he saw there a man who had no wedding garment; and he said to him, 'Friend, how did you get in here without a wedding garment?' And he was speechless. Then the king said to the attendants, 'Bind him hand and foot, and cast him into the outer darkness; there men will weep and gnash their teeth.' For many are called, but few are chosen."[36]

[36] Matt. 21:45—22:14.

⁕

Many of us have pulsing in our heads the verses from Coleridge's "Ancient Mariner" that are, or were until recent reforms in education wiped out learning, a staple of a child's literary education. "The feast is set, the guests are met ..." One can hear the merry din. Weddings are the great feasts of life, even if clergymen may not relish their multiple sequence in the parish calendar. Our Lord sees the whole world as a wedding. His last parable before consummating salvation on the Cross was about the marriage of the king's son.

Some republicans (the small-*r* kind) are confounded when royal funerals, weddings, and golden jubilees draw millions of rapt observers. But the most ardent royalist admits that the messianic kingship is not of this world. Ask Pontius Pilate or the crowd Jesus shunned when they tried to make Him their kind of king in Galilee. The same Temple gathering that heard the parables of the two sons and the wicked husbandmen hears this from the lips of the Heavenly Bridegroom. By the testimony of St. Paul,[37] this man is the Once and Future King and is still King when cloistered in the carpenter's shop, a supernatural version of King Charles hiding in the oak at Boscobel.

[37] Phil. 3.

This parable is added to the pair of warnings about Christ's rejection by the Jews. It would be disloyal to the tribe not to feast, so even in the heaviest private sorrow, the public Jew will "anoint his head and wash his face that he appear not unto men to fast."[38] Christ will raise that etiquette to the holiest pitch when He breaks bread in the Upper Room hours before sweating blood. Those first called, who violated protocol and decency by refusing to attend the wedding, will be replaced by those of lesser rank. So far, the fellows listening in the cheaper seats are gloating at the Pharisees. But for their own obstinacy, they will be cast aside in favor of the lesser breeds outside the Jewish Law. At once the audience shares the unease of the Pharisees, for the Master has shifted into another gear, and they do not know where He is taking them. Those lesser breeds are all of us from China to Canada—and this includes Rome and Dublin. There is only one caste in God's system, and it is the outcast. But raised in dignity, one man refuses to don the ceremonial garment and is cast out, not by men but by God.

From the Missionaries of Charity convent in Harlem, where I used to say Mass, I could watch poor people entering a store-front gospel church dressed in hats and gloves and suits that I rarely saw in rich parishes of Christ's one true Church. Good people the suburban Catholics were, but quick to make worship a dress-down occasion.

Businesses are finding that dressing down for work reduces productivity, and rumor speaks of a return to better days. Even at the Met, the opera hat has been replaced by the baseball cap—although, by some curious transmigration, last summer I also saw a man in a top hat at Yankee Stadium, but he was

[38] Cf. Matt. 6:17–18.

just trying to catch the eye of the camera. My grandfather was a friendly man, but he stopped going to the opera in 1946 when he saw a man there in a brown business suit. My grandfather said it was rude to the singers.

Jesus did not preach this parable on His way to suffering and death in order to give me a platform to rant about haberdashery. But dare I say that our Lord had an eye for clothes? Not always approvingly: He had strictures about broad phylacteries and long tassels. But He wore a seamless garment, which was a fine thing worth gambling for, and His first motion when He rose from the dead was to fold up His grave clothes neatly. Either He did it or an angel, but it evokes a sartorial mystery, stretching from Joseph's colored coat to the white robes of the heavenly martyrs.

Man is to present himself with dignity before the King, and that dignity is not of man's making: "You have not chosen me, but I have chosen you."[39] To deny that is to be denied the feast. This goes even for that eighteenth-century peeress, dressed in idiosyncratic morals, who said: "God would never damn a British duchess."

Fine studies of this parable by evangelical Christians miss the one point that is the whole point—the center of the parable that is also its circumference, rather like God Himself: the wedding feast is the Eucharist, to which we are admitted by baptism, and those baptismal robes are laundered in the confessional and flaunted in all the sacraments. For the Catholic, the wedding garment is worn all the time in the sacramental life. It should not be hidden away in a hope chest for the Last Judgment.

---

[39] John 15:16, Douay-Rheims Bible.

Twelve

≈

The Ten Virgins

"Then the kingdom of heaven shall be compared to ten
maidens who took their lamps and went to meet the
bridegroom. Five of them were foolish, and five were
wise. For when the foolish took their lamps, they took no
oil with them; but the wise took flasks of oil with their
lamps.

"As the bridegroom was delayed, they all slumbered
and slept. But at midnight there was a cry, 'Behold,
the bridegroom! Come out to meet him.'

Then all those maidens rose and trimmed their
lamps. And the foolish said to the wise, 'Give us some
of your oil, for our lamps are going out.'

But the wise replied, 'Perhaps there will not be
enough for us and for you; go rather to the dealers and
buy for yourselves.'

"And while they went to buy, the bridegroom came,
and those who were ready went in with him to the marriage
feast; and the door was shut. Afterward the other maidens
came also, saying, 'Lord, lord, open to us.' But he replied,

'Truly, I say to you, I do not know you.' Watch therefore, for you know neither the day nor the hour."[40]

．＊

If the Basilica of St. Peter in Rome were destroyed by an earthquake, the Catholic Church would go on a bit dusted but without missing a beat. Lost, though, would be any aesthete whose faith was founded on a fondness for the architecture of Michelangelo. I am perhaps belaboring the obvious, but the obvious was hidden to those who promoted Catholicism for every reason except Christ: her buildings, her lands, her crowds, her political influence. The Holy Spirit recently has given the Church a massive purge. The hierarchy and the faithful were taught a lesson in humility when scandals showed how drowsy we are as servants of the Lord. From now on, a miter will convince only if the wearer of the miter convinces; and a Catholic who thought he was such because he called himself Catholic will have to learn anew what it is to confess Christ crucified.

Pomposity animated those who showed our Lord the splendor of the marble buildings in Jerusalem.[41] He loved the Temple, even to the point of cleansing it, but He was not impressed with the Herodian embellishments. It would all come down. The logical question of when this would happen was answered with the parable of the ten virgins.

[41] Matt. 24:1.

John Calvin was not wrong about everything, and he was right in being impatient with esoteric allegorizers who read all sorts of meanings into the lamps and the oil in them and the number of maidens and their virginity. Some of the early exegetes, Eastern and Western, made an art of labyrinthine interpretations, and to the extent that they do not distort the core meaning, they are harmless and even edifying. But a bridge is better built by Roebling than by Rube Goldberg. We shall never know all about these ten lamps, but there are three things we do know and should never lose sight of in the mire of elaborate allegory: their meaning, their reason, and what to do about them.

Their meaning is that the soul must always be prepared. The Church Militant is more specifically like the Marines, whose Latin motto is "Semper fideles." This is not the same as always watching, for the wise sleep as well as the foolish. One kind of sleep is trust, and the other is neglect. When you sleep, you must consecrate your sleep, like Pope John XXIII, who put his guardian angel in charge of the Church when he went to bed. This faith, which is the opposite of presumption, breeds the Romans who say: "When a pope dies, make another." The only popes who would object to that nonchalance are those who were not saints.

The reason for preparation is that we do not know the hour of the Bridegroom's arrival. Demagogues claim they know: the airwaves are laden with the voices of evangelists predicting oceans of blood within the week, and still they accept checks dated later than that. Excitable innocents make the same mistake in their quiet hysteria, using a Lateran Council to warn that the crossbow will end civilization or using modern microphones to compare the Persian Gulf War to Armageddon. There is a difference between holy fear and servile fear, and its name is prudence.

The Ten Virgins

All ten virgins had lamps, but only five lamps were lit. Sanctifying grace has to be kindled by actual graces and frequent confession. The parable speaks to the believer, not to the pagan. Among believers, enthusiasts and formalists share the error of founding faith on something other than the light of Christ. The "born again" Christian who will tell you the hour he was saved is easily lost when he stops feeling saved. The cultural Catholic who lacks the interior strength to pursue the sacramental life justifies himself by saying that he is rejecting "Catholic guilt."

But guilt is not Catholic. Guilt is guilt. The guilty slumber as though life is all a dream, having made no provision for the inevitable confrontation with Truth. When they do come to their senses, the door of reality will be shut in their faces, and like every scorner of the Church, they will blame the Truth for being true.

It is not idle allegory to say that the wise virgins processing to meet the Bridegroom are the Church in eucharistic celebration. The celebrants are those who live day in and day out, knowing that the Truth will appear. This explains the palpable radiance a pastor sees in some very old people who beam at the prospect of seeing God face-to-face. They are not among those burned at the stake or gored by lions. But martyrdom is a bad half hour. Fidelity consists in living the daily routine—if not ground by beasts, then ground down by the daily grind for as long as the Bridegroom wills it—before the heavenly nuptials.

Thirteen

⚜

The Talents

For it will be as when a man going on a journey called
his servants and entrusted to them his property; to one he
gave five talents, to another two, to another one, to each
according to his ability. Then he went away. He who had
received the five talents went at once and traded with them;
and he made five talents more. So also, he who had the two
talents made two talents more. But he who had received the
one talent went and dug in the ground and hid his master's
money.

"Now after a long time the master of those servants came
and settled accounts with them. And he who had received
the five talents came forward, bringing five talents more,
saying, 'Master, you delivered to me five talents; here I
have made five talents more.' His master said to him, 'Well
done, good and faithful servant; you have been faithful over
a little, I will set you over much; enter into the joy of your
master.'

"And he also who had the two talents came forward,
saying, 'Master, you delivered to me two talents; here I

have made two talents more.' His master said to him, 'Well done, good and faithful servant; you have been faithful over a little, I will set you over much; enter into the joy of your master.'

"He also who had received the one talent came forward, saying, 'Master, I knew you to be a hard man, reaping where you did not sow, and gathering where you did not winnow; so I was afraid, and I went and hid your talent in the ground. Here you have what is yours.' But his master answered him, 'You wicked and slothful servant! You knew that I reap where I have not sowed, and gather where I have not winnowed? Then you ought to have invested my money with the bankers, and at my coming I should have received what was my own with interest. So take the talent from him, and give it to him who has the ten talents. For to every one who has will more be given, and he will have abundance; but from him who has not, even what he has will be taken away. And cast the worthless servant into the outer darkness; there men will weep and gnash their teeth.' "[42]

---

[42] Matt. 25:14–30.

⁂

In the line of other parables about productivity (the sower, the mustard seed, and the tares of the field), the parable of the talents[43] could be called "The Industrious and Static Managers."

Much pastoral teaching today is old-fashioned compared with the Bible. Rooted in socialist biases popular in mid-twentieth-century Europe and America, an uninformed model of static economics persists from the pulpit — decades after St. John Paul II's 1991 encyclical, *Centesimus Annus*, reminded the world that wealth is the product not of dead metals, but of human creativity.

Our Lord does not disdain, and even encourages, free enterprise — especially in this parable, in which he uses business as a metaphor for the economy of grace.

A talent is an ancient Greek currency equivalent to the weight in silver of a big *amphora* (storage jug) of water. In the New Testament Holy Land, a full amphora weighed about 130 pounds. At current silver prices, each talent the lord entrusted to his servants was worth nearly $33,000. Wealth of the kind measured in Greek talents needs the addition of human talent to grow.

[43] See also Luke 19:12–27.

But again, all this is really about grace. Like natural resources, graces abound in their variety.[44] The good Christian is a "good steward of the manifold graces of God."[45]

The gift of faith, which comes to us from God, is a sublime grace. But we are not intended to keep it to ourselves — in effect, to bury it in the ground. The apostolic fishermen were ordained to be fishers of souls and not custodians of an aquarium.

The temptation to treat grace as a static commodity is as old as the gift of grace itself. St. Paul regretted that none of the other workers in the field of the Lord could match Timothy's zeal for souls: "They all look after their own interests, not those of Jesus Christ."[46] The apostle scorns the private religiosity of those who think keeping the Faith is justified in itself apart from spreading the Faith. Fidelity is not a spiritual form of intestinal retention.

In the parable, one servant is prevented from investing by servile fear. This is very different from the virtue of *holy* fear, for servility does not trust God. Everyone is given gifts in different measure. What matters is our degree of trust in the divine economy, in which grace builds on grace. Christ does not expect us to be wizards at this. In the economy of that time, a fivefold or tenfold return on investment was not unusual, and doubling was about average. The bottom line is not the amount of grace, but the amount of the self that is invested to spread it. Eternal rewards are commensurate with this self-investment.

Nothing will be entrusted to the untrusting: "If then you have not been faithful in the unrighteous mammon, who will entrust

---

[44] 1 Cor. 12:7–12.
[45] 1 Pet. 4:10, Douay-Rheims Bible.
[46] Phil. 2:21.

to you the true riches?"[47] Servile fear is a projection onto God of the self's own mercilessness toward the self: "I knew you to be a hard man."[48] No one who really knows Jesus knows Him that way. But His truth is harsh when it is up against a lie.

We are unworthy servants but are worth all things to Him nonetheless. The hesitant man will say, "Lord, I am not worthy," but will *not* say, "But only say the word and my soul shall be healed." He cannot then enter into the joy of his Master—which means feasting.[49] Our Lord alludes to the heavenly feast that is communion with God, of which we partake in the Eucharist. Lack of trust in God makes all this impossible, excommunicating the self.

One advertisement for a recent World Youth Day spoke of "celebrating life," "promoting the dignity of the human person," and "building a civilization of love." All well and good. But Christ was not mentioned once, nor was His gospel—because, I was told, there was a fear of alienating nonbelievers.

This may be prudential protoevangelization. But caution is not always prudent. General Rundle "never took a risk and was rewarded by never suffering a reverse." He also never won. At some point, the Lord of Life must be invoked as the cause of celebrating life, and some account must be given of the Source of the dignity being promoted, and someone will have to name the Author of the love that civilizes. I have never known anyone converted by a mere implication, and John Henry Cardinal Newman said that no one is a martyr for a conclusion.

The parabolic investors had to be talented in propagating their talent; they also had to trust in the power of that talent.

[47] Luke 16:12, King James Bible.
[48] Matt. 25:24.
[49] Matt. 25:10.

"For whoever is ashamed of me and my words in this adulterous and sinful generation, of him will the Son of man also be ashamed, when he comes in the glory of his Father with the holy angels."[50]

Our Lord also said — in language perhaps a bit daunting for official World Youth Day T-shirts — that damnation awaits those who call themselves Christians but do not spread His grace. They are fixtures in an unheavenly scene: "waterless clouds, carried along by winds; fruitless trees in late autumn, twice dead, uprooted; wild waves of the sea, casting up the foam of their own shame; wandering stars for whom the nether gloom of darkness has been reserved for ever."[51]

[50] Mark 8:38.
[51] Jude 12–13.

Fourteen

⚜

The Two Debtors

One of the Pharisees asked him to eat with him, and he
went into the Pharisee's house, and sat at table. And behold,
a woman of the city, who was a sinner, when she learned
that he was sitting at table in the Pharisee's house, brought
an alabaster flask of ointment, and standing behind him at
his feet, weeping, she began to wet his feet with her tears,
and wiped them with the hair of her head, and kissed his feet,
and anointed them with the ointment.

Now when the Pharisee who had invited him saw it, he
said to himself, "If this man were a prophet, he would have
known who and what sort of woman this is who is touching
him, for she is a sinner."

And Jesus answering said to him, "Simon, I have some-
thing to say to you."

And he answered, "What is it, Teacher?"

"A certain creditor had two debtors; one owed five
hundred denarii, and the other fifty. When they could not
pay, he forgave them both. Now which of them will love him
more?"

Simon answered, "The one, I suppose, to whom he forgave more."

And he said to him, "You have judged rightly." Then turning toward the woman he said to Simon, "Do you see this woman? I entered your house, you gave me no water for my feet, but she has wet my feet with her tears and wiped them with her hair. You gave me no kiss, but from the time I came in she has not ceased to kiss my feet. You did not anoint my head with oil, but she has anointed my feet with ointment. Therefore I tell you, her sins, which are many, are forgiven, for she loved much; but he who is forgiven little, loves little." And he said to her, "Your sins are forgiven."

Then those who were at table with him began to say among themselves, "Who is this, who even forgives sins?"

And he said to the woman, "Your faith has saved you; go in peace."[52]

---

[52] Luke 7:36–50.

Few vandals in the corridors of history have done as much damage as princes who were not gentlemen. Populations have fled from raucous tyrants. They also frowned at Charles VII when they remembered Louis IX, and at Cardinal Wolsey because he served no majesty higher than his king's. Even in constitutionally unprincely states such as ours, where there are presidents and no purple, there is a general embarrassment when the bully pulpit is used by bullies.

Simon the Pharisee was not a gentleman. He had a gentleman's manners, perhaps. He knew which knife to use but only for the purpose of sticking it into others.

Jesus praised the righteousness of the Pharisees but not Simon's self-righteousness. Simon's sense of entitlement supposed that he was doing Jesus a favor by inviting Him to dine—like those today who think attending Mass is an obligation but not a privilege.

Their attitude has not been helped in the English-speaking world by the translation of the Holy Mass that for decades was recited from the altars following the close of the Second Vatican Council. It seemed designed to dull the people's understanding of the miracle taking place before them on the altar. As the priest faces the people and proffers the consecrated Host—now the

Body of our Lord—and declares "Behold the Lamb of God," the official Latin of the typical Mass text reads: "Domine, non sum dignus ut intres sub tectum meum . . ." The Roman centurion, imperial trumpets notwithstanding, knew himself unworthy to have the Lord come under his roof.[53]

But from 1970 until 2011, the English translation of the centurion's immortal profession of faith was this: "Lord, I am not worthy to receive you." That is something Queen Victoria might have said to Disraeli in one of her more effusive moments.

Simon, not to be confused with Simon of Bethany, thought himself overly qualified to receive Jesus, whom he addresses as Rabbi with palpable irony, as though he were condescending to some ecclesiastical vagrant. The Pharisee is fascinated with Jesus—the way a lepidopterist is with an exotic butterfly—and he invites Jesus to dine with the intention of pinning Him down.

And what was going on in that room? An account of a mission to the Middle East by the Scottish clergyman Andrew Bonar in 1839 recalls: "At dinner at the consul's house at Damietta, we were much interested in observing a custom of the country. In the room where we were received, besides the divan on which we sat, there were seats all round the walls. Many came in, and took their places on these side seats, uninvited and yet unchallenged. They spoke to those at table, on business, or the news of the day; and our host spoke freely to them."

It is a scene much like the one that occasioned the parable of the two debtors. We do not know where Simon's house was, and any identification of the sinful woman with the Magdalene is a romantic stretch, but both are types. Simon is every calculator

---

[53] See Matt. 8:8; Luke 7:6.

who makes an embarrassing show of his belief in his own superiority—and is undone by a man (similar to one described in Kipling's poem "If—") who "can talk with crowds and keep your virtue, or walk with Kings—nor lose the common touch."

The unnamed woman is the iconic shadow of every soul burdened with a public secret. There is no evident explanation for what strikes others as her histrionic devotion to Jesus. Simon is full of world-weary suspicion: "If this man were a prophet, he would have known who and what sort of woman this is who is touching him, for she is a sinner." Since this private thought found its way into St. Luke's Gospel, Simon no doubt aired it publicly later to justify himself—after Christ dashes him with "something" he has to say.[54]

That something is a short parable about a creditor who has a debtor owing five hundred denarii and another owing fifty—neither of whom can pay. The creditor forgives both men's debts. Jesus asks, "Now which of them will love him more?"

Christ is the creditor. The meager fifty that Simon owes will drag him down to moral squalor because he could perform every precept of religion except love. Says our Lord, "Do you see this woman? I entered your house, you gave me no water for my feet, but she has wet my feet with her tears and wiped them with her hair. You gave me no kiss, but from the time I came in she has not ceased to kiss my feet. You did not anoint my head with oil, but she has anointed my feet with ointment."

Christ comes under the roofs of churches many times in our hardened days without finding tears and confession of sin. A broken generation has grown up ignorant of the confessional, asking with Simon's other guests: "Who is this, who even forgives sins?"

[54] Luke 7:40.

The answer is not easy. A popular television cartoon character declared that people who say there are no easy answers aren't looking hard enough. Confession is not easy, but it is simple. He who forgives sins is Christ the High Priest—worshipped by the Church when she is Catholic enough to wash Christ's feet with her tears and anoint them with the luster of His own priesthood.

Fifteen

≫

The Good Samaritan

*And behold, a lawyer stood up to put him to the test, saying,
"Teacher, what shall I do to inherit eternal life?"*

*He said to him, "What is written in the law? How do
you read?"*

*And he answered, "You shall love the Lord your God
with all your heart, and with all your soul, and with all
your strength, and with all your mind; and your neighbor as
yourself."*

*And he said to him, "You have answered right; do this,
and you will live."*

*But he, desiring to justify himself, said to Jesus, "And
who is my neighbor?"*

*Jesus replied, "A man was going down from Jerusalem
to Jericho, and he fell among robbers, who stripped him
and beat him, and departed, leaving him half dead. Now
by chance a priest was going down that road; and when
he saw him he passed by on the other side. So likewise a
Levite, when he came to the place and saw him, passed by
on the other side. But a Samaritan, as he journeyed, came*

to where he was; and when he saw him, he had compassion, and went to him and bound up his wounds, pouring on oil and wine; then he set him on his own beast and brought him to an inn, and took care of him. And the next day he took out two denarii and gave them to the innkeeper, saying, 'Take care of him; and whatever more you spend, I will repay you when I come back.' Which of these three, do you think, proved neighbor to the man who fell among the robbers?"

He said, "The one who showed mercy on him."

And Jesus said to him, "Go and do likewise."[55]

L egend has Alexander the Great giving a beggar command of five cities in response to his plea for five coins: "You ask as a beggar. I give as a king."

A scribe asks Christ the King for the key to eternal life, but he asks like a religious dilettante. Faced with the very smorgasbord of religions spread before him, he requests a little hors d'oeuvre. Had he been truly pious, he would not have asked so petty a question: "Who is my neighbor?"

Like Alexander, Jesus answers with royal largesse, challenging the lawyer to a life of heroic sacrifice. It is possible that this turned the scribe into a great man. But it is also unlikely. Having been bested by Jesus in the first round of questioning, he makes the second query "to justify himself." That is no way to ask the right question or learn from the right answer. But perhaps we should be grateful that he asked.

There is a numbing tendency to trivialize things beloved, and this parable is among the most beloved of them all. The minds that were inspired to print Leonardo's *Last Supper* on tea towels and sculpt the mystically stigmatized St. Francis of Assisi into a garden ornament are quite capable of seeing the parable of the good Samaritan as a salute to the Red Cross. The story should move the heart to good works, but if that is all it does, it is not understood.

The road, as it descends from Jerusalem to Jericho, was notorious for the brigands who hid along the path to waylay travelers; it was called the bloody road. In the parable, it stands for the trail of human complaint, temptation, and woe everywhere and at all times.

The characters are not precise analogues like the various kinds of soil in the parable of the sower. But the beaten traveler is clearly the figure of every man "born in sorrow." Lying there in a heap of bloodied clothes is the whole human race, mugged by the evil one. That victim is a devil's sacrament of the Fall of man. The other figures in the parable are shades and turns of every one of us.

A priest comes down from Jerusalem, vested in his clerical attire—man-made accoutrements of heaven. There are prohibitions in Jewish law against touching a bloody, possibly dead, and therefore "unclean" man before offering a ritual sacrifice in Jerusalem. But this should not prevent the priest from helping the poor traveler, since he is on his way *back* from the Holy City —he has already made his sacrifice.

But he, whose job is to sacrifice blood, does not want to touch more blood. He would afterward have to go through an inconvenient ritual of self-purification. So he continues on his way in a denial of his own dignity. The High Priest of the everlasting covenant tells this story, hymning the glory of priestliness even as He disdains stingy clerisy.

Today, much of the corruption in the Church stems from clerical self-regard. Not long ago, a bishop in a South African province petitioned Rome for permission to incorporate animal sacrifice into the Eucharist, to make the rite more culturally indigenous. Just as astonishing in its way was an American prelate who put on a Green Bay Packers Cheesehead cap as he began his sermon—to ingratiate himself with Packer fans attending his Mass. Heresy is more easily staunched than vulgarity.

Buffoonery in the sacred liturgy is a particularly tasteless and shocking form of clerical triumphalism. The failure of the current liturgy to instill holy fear engenders a priestly smugness so impenetrable that it forgets Christ the King and High Priest being dressed as a clown by Herod Antipas, the prince of banality, on the night before His Crucifixion. Strained bonhomie is not the way to restore the dignity of the priesthood. That can happen only when the priest kneels down to nurse beaten humanity in the gutter of history.

The Levite, careful for the details of the Law, also passes by —even though the Law commanded that a man rescue even his enemy's donkey.[56] In defining the neighbor, Christ fulfills and does not destroy the law and the prophets.[57] But the modern Levite priest, distracted with a head full of annulment cases and chancery meetings, destroys both law and prophets daily when he veers from his path to avoid the battered modern man.

The Samaritan does not come to the rescue like some deus ex machina. He is anything but a god. The outcast Samaritans were pitiless engines of prejudice as much as victims of it, and to hear a Gerizim Samaritan speak of Jerusalem Jews was like hearing a Muslim extremist talk about Jerusalem Jews today, or about Christians anywhere.

The Samaritans were wrong and stubborn, but the Good Samaritan was good for being a man who saw humanity in another man. His practical response to help the poor soul and pay for his care was not the response of an institutional philanthropy.

---

[56] Exod. 23:4–5.
[57] 2 Chron. 28:5–15; Mic. 6:6–8; Hos. 6:9.

Hints of Heaven

In him was the vital good of the human race in its generational struggle against the defacement of the image of God in man. It has been waged since our first ancestors were charmed by a hiss that told them they could be gods themselves.

Sixteen

⁂

The Rich Fool

One of the multitude said to him, "Teacher, bid my brother di-
vide the inheritance with me." But he said to him, "Man, who
made me a judge or divider over you?" And he said to them,
"Take heed, and beware of all covetousness; for a man's life
does not consist in the abundance of his possessions."

And he told them a parable, saying, "The land of a rich
man brought forth plentifully; and he thought to himself,
'What shall I do, for I have nowhere to store my crops?'
And he said, 'I will do this: I will pull down my barns, and
build larger ones; and there I will store all my grain and
my goods. And I will say to my soul, Soul, you have ample
goods laid up for many years; take your ease, eat, drink, be
merry.' But God said to him, 'Fool! This night your soul is
required of you; and the things you have prepared, whose
will they be?'

"So is he who lays up treasure for himself, and is not rich
toward God."[58]

[58] Luke 12:13–21.

$\mathcal{k}$

This chapter is being written by a man who is grateful for having just offered the Holy Sacrifice of the Mass and who is also trying to suppress his customary chagrin at the foul translation he was obliged to use. Today, the opening collect turned the Latin meaning practically upside down, and then a rubric provided the option of a shortened form of the Gospel[59] for those who did not have time to listen to three concluding verses in Matthew's account of the parable of the wedding feast. If only read and not chanted, it would have imposed an extra thirty seconds. Luke does not include those lines, but he follows the parable with other lines equally severe.

It is no doubt paranoia, nurtured by my experience of liturgists, that prompts me to suspect that there is an aversion among them to talk of obedience and banishment to outer darkness, and a tendency to reduce all the parables to Morality Lite, and salvation to sentimental universalism. There may come a time, if inscrutable Providence permits these meddlers to live, when a rubric will drop the word *not* from several of the Ten Commandments—"to save time."

[59] Matt. 22:1–11.

The parable of the rich fool might be subject to similar butchery by cutting out the last sentence: "So is he who lays up treasure for himself, and is not rich toward God." This parable, inseparable from the psychology of prudence and greed, is incomplete unless it is also understood as a hymn of *saving grace*. By contrast, an ethical culturist would keep it on the placid level of the natural virtues, where Christ is in the story simply to illuminate them, showing that keys to proper conduct become keys to heaven.

A pedant, capable of listening to St. Francis's canticle of the animals and responding with Mr. Gradgrind's definition of a horse,[60] hears our Lord preach on the angels and the Holy Spirit and raises his hand to ask a question about the settlement of an estate. He reminds one of the man who asked Maisie Ward,[61] after she had concluded a brilliant speech, "Mrs. Ward, do you have the time?"

At least the man in Jerusalem was impressed enough by Jesus, whom he must have thought a clever chap, that he hoped an opinion might persuade his brother to hand over half an acre. Jesus does not respond with the righteous wrath wherewith he tossed the money changers out of the Temple (update that to ripping out electric votive lights). With the bemusement of a speaker in Hyde Park heckled by a silly remark, He addresses him with studied iciness: "Why, man, who has appointed me a judge to make awards between you?"[62]

Christ's measure of this covetous man is evident when He proceeds to relate a parable about a "fool." He uses the word in

---

[60] See *Hard Times* by Charles Dickens, at the beginning of chapter 2.
[61] Cofounder with her husband, Frank Sheed, of the famous Catholic publisher Sheed and Ward.
[62] Cf. Luke 12:14.

The Rich Fool

just two other parables: the two builders and the ten virgins. As this man counts his success by what he has, rather than what he is, he probably was too obtuse to feel insulted.

The rich fool envisions life with very limited bounds. That, and not his wealth, is what makes him foolish. To gain wealth usually involves industry, intelligence, patience, and frugality. Applied together, these can make a man into a very good man. The trap of foolishness awaits the man who comes to equate one's good with *goods* — just as Adam and Eve fell by believing that *god* could be plural.

The rich fool built bigger barns to store his wealth and would not have understood the counsel of St. Augustine: "You have barns: the bosoms of the needy, the houses of widows, the mouths of orphans and widows."

What the fool discovers is that mortal goods do not confer immortal goodness. He is like Orson Welles's character in *Citizen Kane*, whose silent death is followed by the banging of the auctioneer's hammer: "Going once, going twice, sold." The Chippendale chairs are carted away, his Mercedes glides off with an unsympathetic driver behind the wheel, and rough hands crate the expensive mirror in which he once contemplated his prosperous jowls.

Greed is the desire to have more than another. Covetousness is the desire for what another has, just for the sake of having it. These two moral coagulants are a formula for misery. If a man's definition of his good is that limited, his capacity for self-deception is limitless. A man so deceived can never be happy, since his happiness is posited on the unhappiness of others. It is the opposite of why we were made, which is to give God delight.

Ultimately, the rich fool denies himself the happiness that comes from giving happiness to God. As God is God, He does not need more happiness. So He gives us back multiples of what we give Him. The fool who locks up what he has finds that he is locking himself out of all that God has to offer.

Seventeen

꙳

The Barren Fig Tree

And he told this parable: "A man had a fig tree planted in his vineyard; and he came seeking fruit on it and found none. And he said to the vinedresser, 'Lo, these three years I have come seeking fruit on this fig tree, and I find none. Cut it down; why should it use up the ground?' And he answered him, 'Let it alone, sir, this year also, till I dig about it and put on manure. And if it bears fruit next year, well and good; but if not, you can cut it down.'"[63]

[63] Luke 13:6–9.

⚜

Citing disasters to challenge the doctrine of God's omnipotence and mercy is a commonplace: "Why did God permit such and such if He is what people say He is?"

Jesus is asked about a massacre of Galileans by Pontius Pilate.[64] Now, Pilate was not such a remote aristocrat that he refused to slaughter, and slaughter he did. But by the time the news spread, it may have been exaggerated. He may or may not have actually committed the unspeakable blasphemy of violating the Temple precincts to mingle the blood of his victims with the blood of the sacrificial animals. His instructions from Rome were to keep the lid on that simmering pot. Riotousness was not in keeping with Roman sangfroid, although it was not alien to Roman anger.

Whatever the details, there had been a massacre. The Jews were not all Jobs, and the general tone of the question they ask Jesus is more superior than pathetic: not "Why did God let it happen?" but "What did the Galileans do to deserve it?" Those asking may even have been thrilled to think that they were spared that calamity because they were better.

The Lord of mercy and truth answers with the parable of the barren fig tree, which recalls earlier statements of God's

---

[64] Luke 13:1.

disappointment with man for his disobedience—such as Isaiah's image of the vineyard that produced bad grapes and Jeremiah's seed of promise that grew into a degenerate plant—King David's lineage—before it brought forth the Messiah.

The teller of this parable is the Messiah Himself, so the moral guilt He addresses goes beyond personality to the whole nation. Jesus shows His audience that they are babes in the wood when it comes to the mystery of evil and justification, of righteousness and indolence. One is reminded of the eighty-nine-year-old archbishop, a veteran of World War II, who said of a statement issued by his fellow bishops about war with Iraq that they did not know what they were talking about. It was an instance of a successor of the apostles speaking like the apostles.

Jesus mentions another tragedy: the collapse of the tower of Siloam on eighteen people.[65] What did the victims do to deserve that? After September 11, 2001, most people did not pose the question, if not out of theological modesty, certainly out of decency. Jesus, as the Truth, sees the big picture: All suffering is the calamity of a fallen world, and that world will collapse entirely if it does not accept its Savior. As the perfect parabolist, he puts it more subtly: In a fallen world there will be loss, as innocent branches are pruned in the life of the tree, but the tree must bear the fruit for which it was made, or it will cease to be a tree.

The House of Israel is the tree whose fruit is to be salvation through the Messiah. The whole world is an orchard, but the peculiar tree of Israel is prophetic. As Christians, the judgment is of the Church Jesus entrusted to us. As the Jews had their prophets, so we Christians have had two thousand years of saints. What have we done with our inheritance of their treasury of merit?

[65] Luke 13:4.

The Barren Fig Tree

We cannot merely answer with the playboy who was asked what he did for a living: "I inherit." Much looks barren in the Church today. Jesus who lamented, "Jerusalem! Jerusalem!" may well lament today, "Los Angeles! Los Angeles!" and "Boston! Boston!" and all the cities of our perplexed planet. When Pope John Paul II went to southern California, he was informed that the Catholics there were the best educated and most prosperous the world has known, and he was not overwhelmed. That well-educated and prosperous smugness now haunts the Church, as it did the tower builders of Siloam.

It takes three years to cultivate a fig tree, and for three years our Lord ministered among us. After the dreadful reckoning, the Intercessor offers one more chance. This is our consolation, but it is also our last chance. Then—no excuses.

Fashionable modern victimology, which holds no one accountable for his sins of omission or commission, makes no impression on the divine Victim. A couple of generations ago, more prudent commentators took to heart a line in Sir James M. Barrie's play *Dear Brutus*, whose characters make excuses for themselves only to be told (quoting Cassius's speech to Brutus in Shakespeare's *Julius Caesar*), "The fault, dear Brutus, is not in our stars but in ourselves."

A once vibrant culture is now a "culture of death," committing demographic suicide by contraception and abortion, and moral suicide by atheism distilled into banality. Evil cannot create. Our culture may find itself cursed like the barren fig tree, unless—and this is the heart of the parable—eyes turn to the Tree of Life and the Savior born on its branches.

Eighteen

࿇

The Great Supper

*But he said to him, "A man once gave a great banquet,
and invited many; and at the time for the banquet he sent
his servant to say to those who had been invited, 'Come;
for all is now ready.' But they all alike began to make
excuses. The first said to him, 'I have bought a field, and I
must go out and see it; I pray you, have me excused.' And
another said, 'I have bought five yoke of oxen, and I go to
examine them; I pray you, have me excused.' And another
said, 'I have married a wife, and therefore I cannot come.'*

*"So the servant came and reported this to his master.
Then the householder in anger said to his servant, 'Go out
quickly to the streets and lanes of the city, and bring in the
poor and maimed and blind and lame.'*

*"And the servant said, 'Sir, what you commanded has
been done, and still there is room.'*

*"And the master said to the servant, 'Go out to the
highways and hedges, and compel people to come in, that
my house may be filled. For I tell you, none of those men
who were invited shall taste my banquet.'"*

Hints of Heaven

Now great multitudes accompanied him; and he turned and said to them, "If any one comes to me and does not hate his own father and mother and wife and children and brothers and sisters, yes, and even his own life, he cannot be my disciple. Whoever does not bear his own cross and come after me, cannot be my disciple. For which of you, desiring to build a tower, does not first sit down and count the cost, whether he has enough to complete it? Otherwise, when he has laid a foundation, and is not able to finish, all who see it begin to mock him, saying, 'This man began to build, and was not able to finish.' Or what king, going to encounter another king in war, will not sit down first and take counsel whether he is able with ten thousand to meet him who comes against him with twenty thousand? And if not, while the other is yet a great way off, he sends an embassy and asks terms of peace. So therefore, whoever of you does not renounce all that he has cannot be my disciple.

"Salt is good; but if salt has lost its taste, how shall its saltness be restored?"[66]

---

[66] Luke 14:16–34.

＊

A plaque in a church naming the donor of a larger plaque, which in turn named the donor of a shrine, reminded me recently of how some people do like to be honored for honoring God. One runs the risk of sounding Bolshevik in condemning all titles and honoraria among the faithful. It was said that Soviet egalitarianism replaced first- and second-class railway cars with first- and second-class trains.

Our Lord does make a sharp point about the difference between generosity and calculation. There apparently was an awkward silence when He said, sitting at the table of a Pharisee, that men should not seek places of honor and that charity should be for charity's sake and not for show. A fellow diner changes the subject by turning an aspiration into a bromide: "Blessed is he who shall eat bread in the kingdom of God."[67] He has his modern counterpart in the presumptuous enthusiast who makes a mantra of "Thank ya, Jesus!"—never doubting that he will be at the Table.

Christ the Living Bread never uttered a bromide in His life. His delicate reply—the parable of the great supper—leads the man and the other prosperous diners into a whole new world,

[67] Luke 14:15.

and not one conducive to their digestion. The Kingdom is not as far off as they thought, and as the parable of the barren fig tree portended, places at the heavenly banquet are not guaranteed.

This parable develops the lavish Messianic banquet described by Isaiah[68] in a way different from the parable of the wedding feast,[69] with which it often is conflated. The latter was prelude to the Passion and was addressed to a crowd. But the parable of the great supper is told early in Christ's ministry and is within earshot only of dinner guests. The stubborn guests at the wedding feast were condemned to fire, but here they are just let go, for the Messianic drama has not yet reached the high pitch that three years of preaching will bring.

A wealthy cosmopolitan invites other citizens to a feast ("put it on your calendar"), and when the preparations have been made for those who accepted, there is a second summons like a dinner gong. Dinner is served, but the guests withdraw with excuses. They may have been like those always perched on the lowest rung of social grace, turning down an original invitation in favor of a better one. Or, more consistently with the leitmotif of the parable, they are just indifferent.

This is a parable about people who make every excuse to reject God. Any brush will do to tar Him and His Church. One has a field to inspect, another a new team of oxen, and another has a woman waiting. Today, we might compare these unwilling guests to the nun who decides she can better serve God with an executive salary, the tenure-seeking scholar who will trim his theological sails in the name of academic freedom, or the

[68] Isa. 25:6–9.
[69] Matt. 22:1–10.

adulterer who justifies himself because of a sudden objection to the *homoousian* formula of the Trinity.[70]

Millions of lives have been destroyed by tyrants who excused themselves from the promises once made for them at gleaming baptismal fonts. Countless more souls of God's fair-weather friends have been lost when their faith was rattled by the faithlessness of others. The sybarite, the militant atheist, and the simply lazy soul make a common fraternity when they reject the communion of the Church. Lucifer in all his gaudy horror and the dowdy spiritual couch potato who prefers coffee at home on a cold morning to the Blood of Christ at Holy Mass, sing the same raspy hymn: "They all with one consent began to make excuse."[71]

"There is room for all" in the heavenly banquet, but that does not mean all will find room. Those with excuses will find that there is a lot of room in hellish isolation from God. The guests originally invited are lost, and in their place the Divine Love compels the "poor and maimed and blind and lame" in the lesser lanes of the city: These are the humble who knew they were not what they should be — but who confess their failings. They had kept praying in the back pews as the experts cavorted with balloons and nonsense in the sanctuary.

Then he calls in the virtuous who had not thought of themselves as religious at all. These are the Gentiles in the "highways and hedges" of the whole world, and they come to Christ as many "cradle Catholics" exit the great gothic doors.

[70] The Council of Nicaea declared that Jesus and God the Father are ὁμοούσιος (*homoosian*), or "of the same substance." In English, the Nicene Creed says our Lord is "consubstantial with the Father."

[71] Luke 14:18, King James Bible.

Hints of Heaven

Poulenc's opera *The Dialogue of the Carmelites* is Georges Bernanos's story of the Carmelites of Compiègne who sang the Salve Regina as they went to the guillotine in the French Revolution's Reign of Terror. The executioners and compliant "citizens" had all been baptized, but in the Terror, they excused themselves. I have noticed that the applause at the final curtain usually follows an awkward and solemn silence.

Nineteen

꙳

The Lost Sheep and the Lost Coin

*Now the tax collectors and sinners were all drawing
near to hear him. And the Pharisees and the scribes murmured, saying, "This man receives sinners and eats with
them."*

*So he told them this parable: "What man of you,
having a hundred sheep, if he has lost one of them, does
not leave the ninety-nine in the wilderness, and go after
the one which is lost, until he finds it? And when he has
found it, he lays it on his shoulders, rejoicing. And when
he comes home, he calls together his friends and his neighbors, saying to them, 'Rejoice with me, for I have found
my sheep which was lost.' Just so, I tell you, there will be
more joy in heaven over one sinner who repents than over
ninety-nine righteous persons who need no repentance.*

*"Or what woman, having ten silver coins, if she loses
one coin, does not light a lamp and sweep the house and
seek diligently until she finds it? And when she has found
it, she calls together her friends and neighbors, saying,
'Rejoice with me, for I have found the coin which I had lost.'*

Just so, I tell you, there is joy before the angels of God over one sinner who repents."[72]

[72] Luke 15:1–10.

∗

The parables of the lost sheep and the lost coin mean the same, in the style of Hebrew repetition found especially in the Psalter with couplets such as: "Praise the LORD, all nations! / Extol him, all peoples!"[73] The shepherd who loses one of his hundred sheep and the woman who has ten silver coins, or drachmas, and loses one (approximately a laborer's daily wage) are the same, and what they are is God.

The Pharisees and scribes have murmured of Christ: "This man receives sinners and eats with them." These pompous prigs would have imputed sin to Jesus on the barest suspicion of it, but they had no such suspicion. His most vicious enemies never could find baseness in the Sacred Heart. Their frustration sounds like the political columnist who was so bitterly obsessed with Mother Teresa that he ranted incoherently at her canonization.

To the proud, innocence is more offensive than guilt. Some psycho-biographers have smirked at Mr. and Mrs. Gladstone's endeavors to reclaim fallen women in London, because they were a complicated couple with a lot of mental nooks for neuroses to nest in. In contrast, Dr. Johnson at least once rescued an

[73] Ps. 117:1.

unfortunate woman and nursed her at home, and no one smirked because Johnson, for all his boisterousness, was guileless. No Pharisee could smirk at the motives of Jesus. That may have been the engine of their ultimate rage. They felt so double-crossed by His purity that they sought a solution in the Cross itself.

The sinless Man "received sinners" because His purity was a magnet to those who normally were drawn to their own kind. If the sinners in Galilee had gone to the experts in the Law, they would have left with a lecture on self-improvement ringing in their ears. Jesus simply "received" them. That actually is what happens when we receive Him in Holy Communion. Christ's consorting with sinners who repent is God's side of the Eucharist.

What would be neurotic perfectionism in the imperfect is divine nature in Christ: The least remnant is more important than all the rest. In his retreat for Pope John Paul II, Cardinal Van Thuan said that just as Christ "has no memory" because He forgave the Magdalene and the Thief, so He has no mathematics, because in His equation $1 = 99$. And one coin = nine coins. We should not expect the I AM, the Alpha and the Omega,[74] to have a memory or an imagination as we have it, for He sees all at once.

Nor should we expect the Three-in-One to work by our kind of calculus. As the Holy Trinity is perfect, all external quantities are gratuitous, for God needs nothing and creates for delight rather than to satisfy a need. This is why the "scandal of particularity," which is the problem we have in believing that God, who is greater than the universe, cares for "every hair,"[75] should be the simplest article of faith, not the hardest. But we are procreators

[74] Rev. 1:8.
[75] Cf. Matt. 10:30.

and not the Creator, so we tend to impose the limited logic of our equations on Him.

St. Maximus the Confessor says that Christ's sinlessness did not make Him less human than us, because "sin was not part of the original human condition anyway." Out the window go the pessimistic heresies of human depravity, and the economy of redemption remains. But man is indeed fallen, and in that state his scheme of values is defective.

Our Lord speaks of our best moments, but if they are the best, there are other moments. A priest at an Australian sheep station asked a shepherd's little boy what his own father would do if one of a hundred sheep were lost on a cold night, and the boy replied, "He'd let the little blighter go." And most women would probably not stay up all night looking for a coin. So when Jesus asks, "What man of you ... ?" and "What woman ... ?" he may expect that the people will squirm a little and think to themselves, "Let's not object." Once again He is gently correcting consciences. The difference between Jesus humbling others and the Pharisees humiliating others becomes, after a lifetime, the difference between heaven and hell.

The tears of a good confessor hearing a really contrite penitent are the joy of the shepherd who finds that one sheep and the woman who finds that one coin. This is real "joy in heaven," a mystery more resplendent than satisfaction at finding a lost object or vindication for time spent looking for it. It is the culmination of a mysterious mathematics. St. Josemaría Escrivá said that all of us are zeros, but when Christ is placed in front of all those zeros, what a great number they become.

Twenty

࿊

The Prodigal Son

And he said, "There was a man who had two sons; and the
younger of them said to his father, 'Father, give me the share
of property that falls to me.' And he divided his living between them. Not many days later, the younger son gathered
all he had and took his journey into a far country, and there
he squandered his property in loose living. And when he
had spent everything, a great famine arose in that country,
and he began to be in want. So he went and joined himself
to one of the citizens of that country, who sent him into his
fields to feed swine. And he would gladly have fed on the
pods that the swine ate; and no one gave him anything.

"But when he came to himself he said, 'How many of my
father's hired servants have bread enough and to spare, but I
perish here with hunger! I will arise and go to my father, and
I will say to him, "Father, I have sinned against heaven and
before you; I am no longer worthy to be called your son;
treat me as one of your hired servants." '

"And he arose and came to his father. But while he was
yet at a distance, his father saw him and had compassion,

and ran and embraced him and kissed him. And the son said to him, 'Father, I have sinned against heaven and before you; I am no longer worthy to be called your son.'

"But the father said to his servants, 'Bring quickly the best robe, and put it on him; and put a ring on his hand, and shoes on his feet; and bring the fatted calf and kill it, and let us eat and make merry; for this my son was dead, and is alive again; he was lost, and is found.' And they began to make merry.

"Now his elder son was in the field; and as he came and drew near to the house, he heard music and dancing. And he called one of the servants and asked what this meant. And he said to him, 'Your brother has come, and your father has killed the fatted calf, because he has received him safe and sound.'

"But he was angry and refused to go in. His father came out and entreated him, but he answered his father, 'Lo, these many years I have served you, and I never disobeyed your command; yet you never gave me a kid, that I might make merry with my friends. But when this son of yours came, who has devoured your living with harlots, you killed for him the fatted calf!'

"And he said to him, 'Son, you are always with me, and all that is mine is yours. It was fitting to make merry and be glad, for this your brother was dead, and is alive; he was lost, and is found.' "[76]

[76] Luke 15:11–32.

꙳

Chartres is the cathedral of cathedrals, and here is the parable of parables. Nothing is wanting in the other parables. All are from the lips of the Lord. As one's taste in a certain mood might prefer Cologne or Siena to Chartres, so one might prefer to make a point with the parable of the lost sheep or the lost coin. Those last two parables, followed by the prodigal son, form a triad of responses to the Pharisaic charge: "This man receives sinners and eats with them."

And yet a testimony of sense declares the prodigal son to be "*Evangelium in Evangelio*" — "the Gospel within the Gospel." Its deceptive simplicity will greatly frustrate anyone who thinks he could invent something like it. Try to replicate its spiritual architecture, and you will probably end up with something more like Los Angeles than Chartres. More powerfully and completely than whole libraries of sacred theology, the prodigal son speaks to our mortal mind and heart about why God created mankind and chose to give Himself to us.

By Mosaic Law,[77] the elder son received a double portion of the patrimony, and so the younger son in this parable was content with one-third of the estate, provided he could have it

[77] Deut. 21:17.

immediately. There is nothing coy about our Lord's tone: the father is God, and the sons are shades and shavings of the human soul.

The impetuous son uses his free will. This is not quite what Chesterton had in mind when he wrote, "If a thing is worth doing, it is worth doing badly."[78] If the free will is worth exercising, the poverty and degradation that ensue certainly show that the younger son has "done" his freedom badly.

We are prodigies by grace and prodigals by abuse of grace. In the parable, the final degradation, really a mockery, is to feed pigs. The Levitical code[79] does not see pigs as *Animal Farm*–clever or "Three Little Pigs"–cute. Under Jewish law, pigs are as repulsive as a contagion, and the prodigal son has to feed them, which is even more demeaning than eating them. He finally converts to moral reason when he is tempted by hunger to eat what pigs eat.

We cannot easily sense the impact this image had on the Pharisees and scribes, but before they could do more than raise their eyebrows and suck in their breath, Christ summons all the instruments of His rhetorical symphony. A moral sun shines, and the son prophesies the Catholic act of contrition: he is heartily sorry for his sins (he will confess what he has done against heaven and his father), he does penance (by making the journey home from the far country of shattered illusions), and he will amend his life (volunteering as one of his father's hired servants). When Jesus describes the father running out to meet the son with compassion and joy, you can already see the

---

[78] See G. K. Chesterton, *What's Wrong with the World* (1910), pt. 4, chap. 14.
[79] Lev. 11:7.

wounds in His hands and the light of the Resurrection dawning behind Him: "your brother was dead and is alive again, and was lost and is found."

In my confessional I have an engraving of Tiepolo's painting of this scene. The actual scene is lived out every hour of every day in the confessionals of Catholicism. The son receives a robe and a ring and a feast as tokens of status fully restored. The sacrament of Reconciliation does not just patch us up; it restores the luster of baptismal dignity.

The tragic phrase in the parable is not about the prodigal's debauchery; it is from the elder who cannot bring himself to call his brother his brother. The music and dancing of the world redeemed is to him a profane minstrel show. He speaks to his father icily of "your son." The father's reply thaws that by gently calling him *teknon* ("child"). The Risen Christ will intensify that by calling the bewildered apostles *padeia* ("little children").

Child—he tells him—this my son is your brother: "your brother was dead and is alive again, and was lost and is found." St. Paul, the Apostle to the Gentiles, learned this mercy and said of a sinner, "[Y]ou ought rather to forgive him, and comfort him, lest perhaps such a one should be swallowed up with overmuch sorrow."[80]

Overmuch sorrow. It is a lovely expression we owe to the translators commissioned by King James. And it is also a cruel and haunting thing in fact. The modern age, which, like the prodigal son, wanted everything *modo* ("now"), is still scrambling out of its fatal pigsty. Overmuch sorrow pulls its victims back down. Overmuch sorrow makes it hard to go home from the faraway land of outmoded illusions. Overmuch sorrow makes

[80] 2 Cor. 2:7, King James Bible.

the door of the confessional heavy to open, for fear that a voice inside will be as hard and cold as the shrill modern sirens that led so many to physical and moral death. But when the door is opened, there is "joy in the presence of the angels of God."[81]

---

[81] Luke 15:10, King James Bible.

Twenty-One

ᴊ

The Unjust Steward

He also said to the disciples, "There was a rich man who
had a steward, and charges were brought to him that this
man was wasting his goods. And he called him and said
to him, 'What is this that I hear about you? Turn in the
account of your stewardship, for you can no longer be
steward.' And the steward said to himself, 'What shall I
do, since my master is taking the stewardship away from
me? I am not strong enough to dig, and I am ashamed to
beg. I have decided what to do, so that people may receive
me into their houses when I am put out of the stewardship.'
So, summoning his master's debtors one by one, he said to
the first, 'How much do you owe my master?' He said, 'A
hundred measures of oil.' And he said to him, 'Take your
bill, and sit down quickly and write fifty.' Then he said to
another, 'And how much do you owe?' He said, 'A hun-
dred measures of wheat.' He said to him, 'Take your bill,
and write eighty.'

"The master commended the dishonest steward for his
prudence; for the sons of this world are wiser in their own

generation than the sons of light. And I tell you, make friends for yourselves by means of unrighteous mammon, so that when it fails they may receive you into the eternal habitations.

"He who is faithful in a very little is faithful also in much; and he who is dishonest in a very little is dishonest also in much. If then you have not been faithful in the unrighteous mammon, who will entrust to you the true riches? And if you have not been faithful in that which is another's, who will give you that which is your own?"[82]

[82] Luke 16:1–12.

﷽

Seeking the solace of a cup of tea as I began to write this chapter, I took the first tea bag I could find, and it happened to be the sort of gift the People of God bestow upon their clergy when the ordinary is not good enough. It was "a green tea and herbal infusion" with this written on the packet: "High in the Kunlun Mountains of China, monks spend days chanting and meditating in hopes of reaching complete enlightenment. Periodically they stop for a cup of tea quite like this." I am drinking it even as I write, and it is probably the most ecumenical act I shall commit all year.

The men in the crowd to whom Jesus told the parable of the unjust steward were whole worlds away from the monks of Kunlun. They must have included clever merchants to elicit from the Master this language about shrewd bookkeeping, for He always spoke in images crafted to hit home. They were numbered among the Lord's "disciples" and had been assured in the previous three parables of the Divine Love. Here they are warned not to take for granted that which the Divine Mercy has granted. They are to bask in the love of God, which shines on them only that they might also shine it toward others. Edith Wharton used an Edwardian image when she said that the two ways to shed light are to be the candle or the mirror that reflects the candle. This parable is about how to be the mirror, and that means using all the brains and resources available.

A steward — that is, a businessman in some executive position — had been caught by the equivalent of the SEC. Perplexed when the "rich man" — that is, the head of the firm — demands to see the accounts, the steward acknowledges like any career bureaucrat or academic that he is not strong enough to dig and yet he is ashamed to beg. He arranges with each of his clients to fix their invoices so that they will take care of him when he gets fired. He must have been swindling them all along, and his habit of deceit is now raised to an art.

Here is Tom Sawyer getting someone else to paint the fence. Here is the crafty politician signing pardons on his last day in office. So Tom gets the fence painted and the politician lives in prosperous retirement playing golf with his jet-set ex-cons.

"Where now are the leaders of the nations? . . . The way of knowledge is something they have not known. . . . The sons of Hagar in search of worldly wisdom, the merchants of Midian and Tema, the tale-spinners and philosophers, none of them have found the way to wisdom."[83]

These are not Christ's models of discipleship, for their mammon is the "mammon of unrighteousness," but their shrewdness, not to be confused with slickness, is a model of, well, shrewdness itself. Pascal was shrewd in his calculations of eternity, and Jesus said that serpentine shrewdness should accompany dove-like innocence along the path to the Peaceable Kingdom, where the lion lies down with the lamb.[84]

---

[83] Bar. 3:16, 23, New Jerusalem Bible.
[84] Cf. Matt. 10:16; Isa. 11:6 ff.

The Unjust Steward

Mammon is unrighteous because industry is a mixed bag of idealism and compromise. One can hardly invest in any market without investing indirectly in corruption — but General Booth (founder of the Salvation Army) said that no money is too dirty for the Lord to clean.

The unjust steward hears no praise for his dishonesty. He is praised for his cleverness, which here means foresight. The heart's longing for heaven — or what bloated theological tracts call the "eschatological consciousness of the human person" — makes saints the most useful citizens on earth. The vision of glory, and the detection of it in each soul, is what makes the young care for aging parents with love and sacrifice, see the retarded child as a gift, and even die on the battlefield for noble causes. It has built the treasures of the Church, and lack of it in our days has despoiled those treasures.

Archbishop Hugo of Rouen told Bishop Thierry of Amiens of the great cathedral builders: "They admit no one into their Company unless he has been to confession." The Church is the shrewdest of all institutions and has outlived all others because she is born of an unearthly innocence. This needs the balance of Clement and Augustine and Bonaventure, or else the consort of shrewdness and innocence twists into a corruption of malice and naiveté.

The Church is the world's practical monitor, and she speaks through solemn priests opening heavenly gates and not hysterical eunuchs guarding a forbidden city. Should she abandon her gifts of theological system, she would utter romance without reason and sentiment without love.

Twenty-Two

⚜

Dives and Lazarus

"There was a rich man, who was clothed in purple and fine linen and who feasted sumptuously every day. And at his gate lay a poor man named Lazarus, full of sores, who desired to be fed with what fell from the rich man's table; moreover the dogs came and licked his sores. The poor man died and was carried by the angels to Abraham's bosom. The rich man also died and was buried; and in Hades, being in torment, he lifted up his eyes, and saw Abraham far off and Lazarus in his bosom. And he called out, 'Father Abraham, have mercy upon me, and send Lazarus to dip the end of his finger in water and cool my tongue; for I am in anguish in this flame.'

"But Abraham said, 'Son, remember that you in your lifetime received your good things, and Lazarus in like manner evil things; but now he is comforted here, and you are in anguish. And besides all this, between us and you a great chasm has been fixed, in order that those who would pass from here to you may not be able, and none may cross from there to us.'

"And he said, 'Then I beg you, father, to send him to my father's house, for I have five brothers, so that he may warn them, lest they also come into this place of torment.'

"But Abraham said, 'They have Moses and the prophets; let them hear them.'

"And he said, 'No, father Abraham; but if some one goes to them from the dead, they will repent.'

"He said to him, 'If they do not hear Moses and the prophets, neither will they be convinced if some one should rise from the dead.' "[85]

[85] Luke 16:19–31.

＊

As this parable of Lazarus is the only one with a proper name, some have thought it an actual account. You might as well say the same of "Jack and the Beanstalk." Lazarus was a name common enough, although events leading to the Passion will give it a solemn timbre.[86] Is our Lord pointing back to what lies ahead, with a gesture only the eternal I AM can manage? He may be referring to His friend, which is more likely than referring to Himself. Using one of the Jewish metaphors for heaven, the Lazarus of the parable will rest "in the bosom of Abraham," and the I AM was before Abraham.

Lazarus is the image of suffering mankind. Dives is the image of indolent mankind, and his name does not appear at all in the actual parable, being assumed only in medieval commentaries. *Dives* is Latin for "rich." However, pilgrims in Jerusalem may still see the House of Dives, just as they may see the Inn of the Good Samaritan on the Jericho Road, and they are of equal archaeological irrelevance. There are carvings of Dives in Sainte-Marie-Madeleine at Vézelay and the Abbey of Saint-Pierre at Moissac, and they are imaginative.

[86] See John 12:9–11.

Contrary to the prejudice of dialectical economists, *dives* means rich in a way that can be good or bad. It means something good in the encyclical *Dives in Misericordia*: God richly offers His mercy to all. The election of the Jews is a sign of that, and Dives, although the encyclical does not say it, is the elect Jew. That does not mean that the earthly good fortune and eternal misfortune of Dives is the fate of the Jew. This parable is for every man, just as "the mystery of election refers to every man and woman."[87]

But it is preached with import for the immediate audience, and so St. Gregory the Great identified Dives with the Jews who "have Moses and the prophets" and Lazarus with the Gentiles who have only the echoes of Sinai in the philosophers and their virtues.

Moralizers would make the rich man and the poor man a poster for economic justice. I have come across a ballad, "Dives and Lazarus," recorded by Mr. and Mrs. Gabriel Coates at Flag Pond, Tennessee, in 1916. Mr. and Mrs. Coates apparently felt against the rich man and for the poor man, and they were not the only ones: their ballad dates back to Elizabethan forms. Charles Dickens gently gives his salute to Lazarus in the life of Christ (*The Life of Our Lord*), which he wrote for his own children in 1849. He surely based *A Christmas Carol* on the unfulfilled plea of Dives to send Lazarus back to the land of the living to give warning. The ghost of Jacob Marley incants to the trembling Scrooge: "Charity, mercy, forbearance, and benevolence were all my business. The dealings of my trade were but a drop of water in the comprehensive ocean of my business!"

Dives had little charity, mercy, forbearance, and benevolence, and his character is thinly drawn, save that it is wrapped in

[87] *Dives in Misericordia*, no. 4.

expensive purple, but he may have had more than some think. Lazarus, covered with untended sores, was left at the rich man's gate each day, presumably because there was some largesse to be expected. The family of Lazarus may have been as heartless as Dives. Lazarus bore on his weary frame the agony of real poverty, and possibly his friends and family deposited him at the rich man's gate to rid themselves of him. Mother Teresa used to say that loneliness is the worst poverty.

The parable is about wealth and poverty, but not just that, and it is about social rejection and acceptance, but not just that. Rich and poor, Jew and Gentile are equally accountable. The social crime of Dives in his luxury turned fatal when it became contempt for eternity. His wealth created the illusion of self-sufficiency. So may the Catholic, who luxuriates in the fullness of truth, wallow in grace until he takes it for granted, "keeping the faith" without spreading it — going to church without tending the souls starving for the Lord of Life in a culture of death.

"There is a great gulf fixed ..."[88] That is one of the most daunting lines from the lips of Christ. Hell is real, and there really is a particular judgment of each soul.[89]

Christ calls in love to each soul. It is a warning and not an assurance. The gates of heaven will not open to those who shut their own gates in this world.

[88] Luke 16:26, King James Bible.
[89] Cf. 2 Cor. 5; Phil. 1:21 ff.; Heb. 9:27.

Twenty-Three

⁂

The Unjust Judge

And he told them a parable, to the effect that they ought always to pray and not lose heart. He said, "In a certain city there was a judge who neither feared God nor regarded man; and there was a widow in that city who kept coming to him and saying, 'Vindicate me against my adversary.' For a while he refused; but afterward he said to himself, 'Though I neither fear God nor regard man, yet because this widow bothers me, I will vindicate her, or she will wear me out by her continual coming.'"

And the Lord said, "Hear what the unrighteous judge says. And will not God vindicate his elect, who cry to him day and night? Will he delay long over them? I tell you, he will vindicate them speedily. Nevertheless, when the Son of man comes, will he find faith on earth?"[90]

---

[90] Luke 18:1–8.

⁂

The driver's license registration hall of the Department of Motor Vehicles (DMV) is a great equalizer. All classes, ages, and races huddle together on the benches. A rich man cannot send his chauffeur as a surrogate. Even if you live in New York City, where a driver's license is largely symbolic for those without cars, you still have to show up before (as the clerk ominously says) "the day you expire." And unlike Almighty God, the DMV actually gives you an expiration date.

My recent experience there was like a more enjoyable version of the last moments on the *Lusitania*.[91] It was also very unlike the court of the Unjust Judge,[92] whose abuse of justice lacked the even-handed, roulette-wheel caprice of New York's DMV. As an Oriental arbiter of human fate, the judge traveled about with his collapsible tent and made it known that a bribe (and only a bribe) was surety for a hearing.

Our modern, litigious society should not think itself superior. Like our vast legal culture, the parabolic judge regarded neither God nor man. He was a secularist and an egoist and thus

---

[91] That was a British ocean liner (Cunard Lines) sunk in 1915 by a German torpedo.

[92] Luke 18:1–8.

defied the two highest commandments—to love God and your neighbor. But his indifference showed not the lack of human respect that should animate a judge—who should make decisions without concern for what other men think. He had much human respect—all of it focused on him.

A painting of the parable by John Everett Millais around 1860 shows a flaccid voluptuary enthroned on pillows. When Justice Oliver Wendell Holmes said that he did not do justice, he just did the law, at least he did not do Oliver Wendell Holmes. The prejudice of his legal positivism notwithstanding, he did not lie about on satin pillows fanning away people of no profit to him.

An oppressed woman who approaches, seeking justice, is female and poor and thus at a double disadvantage in the perfumed audience hall. She has only persistence on her side. I do not know whether she is more like the telemarketer or like the atonal parishioner who thinks that if she asks enough, she can sing at her daughter's wedding. Perhaps she is neither. Our Lord gives us to understand that she seeks justice rightly, having been wronged. The woman keeps coming at the judge, and finally he relents. She *importunes* the judge. It is a nice term, and one that suited a quieter English-speaking world—before the advent of telephone calls at two in the morning.

The woman's importuning was more violent than the translations commonly render when they say that she might "wear out" the judge. The Greek word is a boxing term. The plump judge on his couch fears that she will disfigure his face and give him a black eye. We may assume that the judge's verdict was just—because the widow's cause was just and his injustice was a matter of luxury and not jurisprudence.

Some parables are allegorical, but not this one. Our one God is not an unjust judge who will be awakened by a pagan Greek who finally calls the right name into the Pantheon; nor is He so serene that only a Hindu prayer wheel can awaken Him. Jesus tells this parable "to the effect that they ought always to pray and not lose heart."

Discouragement literally means losing heart. It drives the recidivist who is a potential saint away from his next confession; the driver is the Liar. God knows every prayer before we pray and answers every prayer before we start complaining.

This parable is a brilliant varnish on Christ's reminder that a father does not give his son a stone for bread or a snake for fish.[93] It is fashionable to disparage the arm-twisting kinds of petitions that beleaguered souls make in desperate moments. I suppose more people pray to St. Jude and St. Anthony than to St. Maximus the Confessor and the Venerable Bede.

But these saints, and all the rest of those in white robes, intercede before God, who wants us to persevere in prayer only that we might see how He has answered our petitions or increased our faith like Jacob[94] and the Syrophoenician woman.[95] A parish priest may want some of his flock to be less demanding of our great God, but when he opens each week the petition box, he reads some requests that would move even a busy man to tears.

Christ wants us to keep asking until we realize that He has answered our prayers in the way that will make us suppliants happy—not until the next mortgage payment or the clean bill of health, but forever. He asks, "When the Son of Man comes, shall He find that faith?" Note the definite article, which is dropped

[93] Matt. 7:9–11.
[94] Gen. 32:21–30.
[95] Mark 7:24–30.

from wanton translations. "That" faith is the faith that persists until the Son of Man, whom our human ego treats like a puppet, comes robed in light as our Savior and King.

Twenty-Four

࿆

The Pharisee and the Publican

*And to some who trusted in themselves as just, and
despised others, he spoke also this parable:*

*"Two men went up into the temple to pray: the one
a Pharisee, and the other a publican.*

*"The Pharisee standing, prayed thus with himself:
O God, I give thee thanks that I am not as the rest of
men, extortioners, unjust, adulterers, as also is this publican. I fast twice in a week: I give tithes of all that I possess.*

*"And the publican, standing afar off, would not so much
as lift up his eyes towards heaven; but struck his breast, saying: O God, be merciful to me a sinner.*

*"I say to you, this man went down into his house justified
rather than the other: because every one that exalteth himself, shall be humbled: and he that humbleth himself, shall
be exalted."*[96]

---

[96] Luke 18:9–14.

M iguel de Unamuno said that a temple is the place where people go to weep. If all the tears shed in a parish church could be bottled, I think the oceans would look small. All tears. Not only of grief. Some are shed raucously at weddings and more softly when a baby is held over the baptismal font. But the greatest tears are in confession.

Jesus told a parable about two men in the Temple, only one of whom wept. He was a sinner, in Roman law a publican commissioned to collect public revenues—and in fact a rapacious man and a collaborator with the Jews' occupying enemy. When I was a child, the son of a family of fixed political loyalties, I misunderstood the sermon about the Pharisee and publican and heard that Jesus approved the prayer of a *Republican*, although it seemed odd that a Republican favored higher taxes.

The publican was a sinner and had yet to put action into his faith. The Pharisee was not a sinner in the way of common sins, but he had yet to put faith into his action.

Here is the old faith-versus-works quarrel, which will be fought so long as the two are posed as opposites. The Pharisee's small soul lacked the élan to know how to be forgiven big. Pride is shameless in its shameful underestimation of grace. The Pharisee might have given Jesus a polite nod, but he could never have washed His feet with tears, and he could not love much, because he had not been forgiven much.

The Pharisee went to the Temple to boast, like those who go to funerals to praise the dead and by so doing smile at death with nervous bravado. The Temple was the Pharisee's sounding board and its arches a frame for his virtue. St. John Climacus called pride the annihilation of virtue. The Pharisee "trusted in himself and despised others." He thanked God that he was better than the publican. It was not gratitude. It was self-canonization, and self-canonization ends with the self, for the self has not the metaphysics to haul itself up to the holy altars.

Priests hear the familiar refrain, "I'd go to confession, but I don't know what to confess." If we examined our own consciences as thoroughly as we examine those of others and followed the penances we mentally prescribe for others, all of us would be dancing with the saints. The pedantic Pharisee simply misses the holy dance and dances with himself in imitation of bliss. He strides boldly through the sanctuary while the publican is "standing afar off."

In today's terms, the Pharisee leaves out the penitential rite, makes the Sign of Peace the climax of worship, and dons the leotard of the liturgical dancer and the jolly red nose of the liturgical clown. The Pharisee might have done the same, had he not been saved by his Oriental dignity, which has left us in our own day.

The publican dares not raise his bloodshot eyes to the blinding glory of heaven. He is both the mystical Byzantine and the critical Latin. He is a sinner, and he knows it, sensing a splendor that the miniature mind of the puffed-up Pharisee missed. Both have souls, but only the publican knows what his soul can yet be. The Pharisee's charade of holiness struts like Napoleon who, as Victor Hugo said, "embarrassed God." Sins hurt the Divine Mercy, but the chief sin of pride is immeasurably worse, for it embarrasses the Divine Majesty.

Jesus says that the sinner beat his breast. The Eucharistic liturgy enjoins a beating of the breast in the penitential rite.

The Puritan divine John Bunyan would have fled the Mass, but he knew this gesture well:

> Smiting upon the breast, seems to intimate a quarrel with the heart for beguiling, deluding, flattering, seducing, and enticing of him to sin: For as conviction for sin begets in man, I mean if it be thorough, a sense of the sore and plague of the heart. So repentance, if it be right, begets in the man an outcry against the heart.... Indeed, one difference between true and false repentance lieth in this. The man that truly repents crieth out of his heart; but the other, as Eve, upon the serpent, or something else. And that the Publican perceived his heart to be naught I conclude, by his smiting upon his breast.

This is the twenty-fourth, and last, of the holy parables. In these chapters, I hope I have not embarrassed God by writing of these majesties each in a few hundred words. Eternity may be long enough to measure all that is in those stories, but there will be no need for any parables if we should be allowed to see the Master face-to-face.

✤

About the Author

Father George W. Rutler is a parish priest in Manhattan and has served in neighborhoods including Park Avenue, "Hell's Kitchen," and the Garment District. The author of eighteen books, he holds degrees from Dartmouth, Johns Hopkins, Rome, and Oxford.

Father Rutler is well known internationally for his programs on EWTN—including *Christ in the City* and *The Parables of Christ*. He originally wrote the chapters of *Hints of Heaven* as a series of articles for *Crisis Magazine*.

An Invitation

Reader, the book that you hold in your hands was published by Sophia Institute Press. Sophia Institute seeks to nurture the spiritual, moral, and cultural life of souls and to spread the Gospel of Christ in conformity with the authentic teachings of the Roman Catholic Church.

Our press fulfills this mission by offering translations, reprints, and new publications that afford readers a rich source of the enduring wisdom of mankind.

We also operate two popular online Catholic resources: CrisisMagazine.com and CatholicExchange.com.

Crisis Magazine provides insightful cultural analysis that arms readers with the arguments necessary for navigating the ideological and theological minefields of the day. *Catholic Exchange* provides world news from a Catholic perspective as well as daily devotionals and articles that will help you to grow in holiness and live a life consistent with the teachings of the Church.

Sophia Institute Press also serves as the publisher for the Thomas More College of Liberal Arts and Holy Spirit College. Both colleges provide university-level education under the guiding light of Catholic teaching. If you know a young person seeking a college that takes seriously the adventure of learning and the quest for truth, please bring these institutions to his attention.

www.SophiaInstitute.com
www.CatholicExchange.com
www.CrisisMagazine.com